Navigating Cybersecurity

Defending Against Cyber Threats:
Strategies for a Secure Online Environment

Olivia Larson

Table of Contents

INTRODUCTION

Our lives are now deeply intertwined with the digital world, and technology's power has given us access to unparalleled levels of convenience, connectivity, and creativity. The increasing danger of cyber threats is the dark side of this digital revolution, though. The world of cyberspace is filled with potential threats that can disrupt, compromise, and damage, from shady hackers to highly developed criminal organizations and even state-sponsored entities.

Welcome to "Navigating Cybersecurity: Defending Against Cyber Threats - Strategies for a Secure Online Environment." In the following pages, we'll set out on a journey into the complex field of cybersecurity, learning adversaries' tactics and examining the methods that can help you confidently negotiate this digital battlefield. Cyber threats are no longer only a thing of science fiction; they are now everywhere. They can destabilize countries, destroy businesses, invade people's privacy, and create unimaginable amounts of devastation. Not whether we will face these threats, but rather when and how. It's a brand-new kind of arms race—a race for information, attentiveness, and digital security.

This e-book will give you the information and resources you need to create a stronghold in the online environment. This e-book has much to offer whether you're an individual looking to protect your personal information, a business owner protecting sensitive data, or a curious mind wanting to learn the workings of cyberwarfare.

We will start our adventure by exploring the various types of cyberthreats that lurk in the background and looking at their potential consequences. From there, we'll lay the groundwork for cybersecurity basics, the guiding ideas that serve as the cornerstone of a safe online presence.

The complexity of network security, data protection, web security, and the particular difficulties brought on by mobile devices and cloud computing will be covered in later chapters. We'll go into the world of incident response and recovery, probe into the world of identity and access management, and look into the future to see the trends that will influence the cybersecurity environment.

However, this e-book covers more than just algorithms and encryption keys. Additionally, it deals with the legal and ethical challenges of living in the digital age. We'll explore the shared accountability of governments, corporations, and individuals in the battle against cybercrime and the difficulties of data privacy rules. Remember that cybersecurity is not just the domain of specialists and professionals as we proceed through these chapters. Every individual who clicks a link, writes a password, or connects to the internet must actively participate in this endeavor since it is a group effort. By the time you get to the last page of this e-book, you'll have gained confidence in your ability to contribute to a secure online environment and valuable strategies.

So, let's start this journey together, whether you're a computer enthusiast or a digital newbie, a corporate executive or a concerned parent. We can improve our defenses and prevail in the fight against cyber threats by approaching the digital frontier with the correct knowledge and mindset.

CHAPTER I

Understanding Cyber Threats

Different Types of Cyber Threats (Malware, Phishing, Ransomware, etc.)

In the ever-evolving landscape of the digital age, our interconnected world presents a host of opportunities and conveniences. Yet, as we navigate this virtual realm, we must also be acutely aware of the lurking shadows that threaten our cybersecurity. From malicious software to cunning manipulation, cyber threats manifest in various forms, each with the potential to disrupt, compromise, and inflict substantial harm. This section aims to shed light on some of the most pervasive types of cyber threats, exploring the mechanics behind them and the strategies required to thwart their advances.

At the forefront of cyber threats stands malware, a catch-all term for various malicious software designed to infiltrate systems, steal data, or cause harm. Among the many forms of malware are Trojan, worms, viruses, and spyware. Viruses attach themselves to legitimate files and replicate as those files are shared, while worms are standalone entities that self-propagate through networks. Trojans masquerade as harmless software but harbor malicious intent, and spyware stealthily collects sensitive information. These stealthy invaders often exploit vulnerabilities in software or human behavior to gain access, emphasizing the critical importance of regular updates, strong firewalls, and robust security software.

In psychological manipulation, phishing emerges as a particularly insidious cyber threat. Operating under the guise of legitimate communication, phishing attacks deceive recipients into revealing sensitive information, such as passwords, credit card details, or personal identifiers. Attackers craft convincing emails or messages that mimic trusted entities, coercing recipients to click on malicious links or download harmful attachments. This exploitation of human psychology, often fueled by urgency or fear, underscores the need for vigilant skepticism and awareness. Verifying the authenticity of requests and scrutinizing URLs before sharing information can serve as effective defenses against this form of cyber deceit.

Ransomware catapults cyber threats to a more visceral level, locking individuals, businesses, and even government entities out of their own data until a ransom is paid. This attack encrypts critical files and demands payment in exchange for the decryption key. The implications are profound, as organizations may face operational paralysis and data loss, leading to significant financial and reputational damage. Notorious incidents, such as the WannaCry attack, have highlighted the far-reaching consequences of ransomware. Prevention and preparation are key in countering this threat. Regular backups, secure software practices, and a robust incident response plan can mitigate the impact of ransomware attacks.
Distributed Denial of Service (DDoS) attacks reign supreme in the realm of disrupting online services. These attacks involve overwhelming a target server, website, or network with an avalanche of traffic, rendering the service inaccessible to legitimate users. The traffic surge originates from a network of compromised devices, often

forming a "botnet." This army of hijacked devices acts in concert to flood the target with traffic, causing a debilitating slowdown or complete shutdown. DDoS attacks have been used for various purposes, from hacktivism to extortion. Mitigation strategies include traffic filtering, load balancing, and building robust network infrastructure.

Beyond exploiting technological vulnerabilities, cyber threats frequently use the human element through social engineering. Attackers trick individuals into divulging sensitive information or doing actions that compromise security by preying on human psychology and trust. Techniques such as pretexting (creating fabricated scenarios to extract information), baiting (luring victims into downloading malware), and tailgating (gaining unauthorized physical access) illustrate the diverse tactics of social engineering. As technology advances, cultivating a strong sense of skepticism and ongoing education and awareness campaigns becomes paramount in guarding against these manipulative tactics.

As we navigate the digital landscape, understanding the varied forms of cyber threats is pivotal to mounting an effective defense. Malware, phishing, ransomware, DDoS attacks, and social engineering represent just a fraction of the arsenal wielded by cyber adversaries. Vigilance, education, and a proactive approach to cybersecurity are essential components of safeguarding our interconnected world. We may reduce the risks presented by these widespread and constantly changing cyber threats by arming ourselves with information and encouraging a culture of security, guaranteeing a more secure and safer online environment for ourselves and generations to come.

Real-world Examples of High-Profile Cyber Attacks

In the interconnected landscape of the modern world, where digital systems underpin critical infrastructure, commerce, and communication, the specter of cyber attacks looms large. From government institutions to multinational corporations, no entity is immune to the far-reaching impact of these attacks. This section delves into some of the most significant and high-profile cyber attacks that have reverberated globally, illuminating the strategies employed by attackers and the lessons they offer for the ongoing battle to secure the digital frontier.

One of the most groundbreaking and mysterious cyber attacks in history, Stuxnet emerged as a harbinger of a new era of warfare: the realm of digital weaponry. Discovered in 2010, Stuxnet targeted Iran's nuclear program by infiltrating industrial control systems. Designed to manipulate centrifuges used in uranium enrichment, this worm covertly disrupted operations, causing physical damage to the centrifuges themselves. Stuxnet underscored the potential for cyber attacks to leap from the virtual world into the physical, demonstrating that the digital realm had become a theater for geopolitical power struggles.

In 2014, Sony Pictures Entertainment fell victim to a cyber attack that went beyond financial implications. This attack, attributed to North Korean hackers, exposed sensitive data, including unreleased films, internal communications, and employee information. Threats of violence accompanied the breach if Sony released the film "The Interview," a satirical take on North Korean leadership. The incident highlighted the intertwining of technology, politics, and freedom of expression, as well as the potential for cyber attacks to disrupt financial stability and cultural diplomacy.

A significant data breach at the major credit reporting agency Equifax in 2017 resulted in the exposure of roughly 147 million individuals personal data. Social Security numbers, birth dates, and financial records were among the data compromised, potentially leading to identity theft and financial fraud. The breach was attributed to a vulnerability in the company's web application software. The Equifax incident starkly demonstrated the cascading repercussions of poor cybersecurity practices, prompting urgent conversations about data privacy, regulatory oversight, and the responsibilities of custodians of personal information.

In 2017, the NotPetya ransomware attack wreaked havoc on organizations worldwide. Disguised as ransomware, NotPetya was designed to irreversibly destroy data, rendering systems inoperable. While it initially appeared as a traditional ransomware attack, it was later revealed to be a "wiper" attack, targeting Ukraine and causing collateral damage to global organizations. The attack highlighted the potential for cyber incidents to escalate into broader geopolitical conflicts, as Ukraine accused Russia of orchestrating the attack as part of a wider campaign of aggression.

The SolarWinds supply chain attack, discovered in late 2020, revealed the extent to which sophisticated attackers could exploit trusted software vendors to infiltrate high-profile targets. Attackers inserted malicious code into SolarWinds' widely used Orion software, which was then distributed to customers, including government agencies and Fortune 500 companies. The attack, attributed to a state-sponsored group, demonstrated the potency of stealthy espionage tactics and the challenges in defending against attacks originating from trusted sources.

These real-world examples of high-profile cyber attacks offer profound insights into the evolving nature of digital warfare. They underscore the far-reaching implications of cyber attacks, transcending mere financial losses to impact diplomacy, privacy, and national security. Furthermore, they emphasize the interconnectedness of our global systems, where vulnerabilities in one corner of the world can ripple across continents.

As defenders of the digital realm, these cases call for a multifaceted response. Investment in robust cybersecurity practices, regular system updates, and continuous monitoring are critical. Equally important is international cooperation, where governments, private sector entities, and individuals collaborate to share threat intelligence and enhance resilience.

In the ever-shifting landscape of cyber attacks, knowledge is a potent defense. By dissecting the strategies and consequences of these high-profile incidents, we empower ourselves to adapt, innovate, and collectively build a more secure digital future. As technology advances, the lessons from these cases serve as beacons, guiding us toward a safer and more resilient cyber landscape.

The Motives Behind Cyber Attacks (Financial, Political, Ideological, etc.)

In the intricate tapestry of the digital age, where information flows ceaselessly across borders and systems, the motives driving cyber attacks are as diverse and complex as the technology itself. Behind each line of malicious code lies a web of intent, a purpose that ranges from financial gain to political manipulation, ideological fervor to espionage. This section delves into the multifaceted motives behind cyber attacks, revealing the motivations that propel attackers and the intricate dynamics that shape the digital battleground.

One of the most prevalent motives driving cyber attacks is the prospect of financial gain. From individual hackers seeking quick profits to sophisticated criminal organizations orchestrating large-scale heists, the allure of monetary rewards fuels a plethora of attacks. These attacks manifest as ransomware, where victims are extorted to pay a ransom to release their encrypted data, or as financial fraud schemes, such as stealing credit card information or engaging in cryptocurrency theft. The potential for substantial profits in the digital realm has turned cybercrime into a lucrative and often well-organized enterprise.

Cyber attacks have become a favored tool for state-sponsored actors engaged in political espionage. To gain an advantage in global affairs, governments often employ cyber attacks to infiltrate rival nations' systems, steal sensitive information, and manipulate public perception. Notable instances include the alleged interference in the 2016 U.S. presidential election and the suspected involvement of nation-states in infiltrating critical infrastructure. These attacks blur the lines between conventional warfare and digital conflict, illustrating the potential for cyber attacks to reshape the geopolitical landscape.

Some cyber attacks transcend financial or political motives, driven instead by ideology and activism. Hacktivist groups, motivated by a sense of justice or the desire to advocate for specific causes, employ cyber attacks to raise awareness, disrupt systems, or expose perceived wrongdoings. For instance, distributed denial of service, or DDoS, attacks on government-owned websites and data breaches aimed at organizations with a contentious agenda. While hacktivism can shed light on important social and political issues, it also raises ethical questions about the means to achieve these ends.

Corporate espionage via cyber attacks has become a significant concern in the competitive landscape of the business world. Rival companies may seek a competitive edge by infiltrating competitors' systems to steal proprietary information, research, and trade secrets. The potential for significant financial gain through intellectual property theft incentivizes attackers to exploit vulnerabilities and employ advanced techniques to breach target organizations. Such attacks underline the need for robust cybersecurity measures to safeguard valuable assets.

As technology evolves, so does the nature of warfare. Cyber attacks have emerged as a powerful tool in the arsenal of nation-states engaged in conflict. From disrupting communication networks to crippling critical infrastructure, the potential impact of cyber warfare is vast. These attacks can weaken adversaries without direct military engagement, leading to a paradigm shift in strategic warfare. Cyberattacks' complexity and covert nature can make attribution challenging, blurring the lines between conventional and digital warfare.

The motives behind cyber attacks form a rich and intricate mosaic, woven from various factors, including financial incentives, political agendas, ideological fervor, and geopolitical power dynamics. The digital age has granted individuals and organizations unprecedented capabilities to wield influence, sow chaos, and achieve their objectives through cyberspace. As technology advances, the motives driving cyber attacks will evolve in tandem, creating a complex and ever-changing landscape that demands vigilance, cooperation, and adaptability from defenders and policymakers alike.

By understanding the motives that underpin cyber attacks, we gain insights into the shifting currents of the digital battlefield. While cyber attacks present challenges, they also offer opportunities for collaboration, innovation, and cultivating a more secure digital environment. As we navigate this dynamic terrain, a comprehensive approach encompassing technological defenses, international cooperation, and ethical considerations will be pivotal in shaping the future of cybersecurity.

CHAPTER II

Fundamentals of Cybersecurity

Confidentiality, Integrity, and Availability (CIA Triad)

The ideas of Confidentiality, Integrity, and Availability (CIA) serve as the cornerstone of cybersecurity in the quickly changing environment of the digital era, where information is a currency and data breaches have the power to destroy economies as a whole. The CIA Triad forms the core framework for assessing and implementing effective security measures in the digital realm. This section delves into the essential concepts of Confidentiality, Integrity, and Availability, exploring their significance, practical applications, and the delicate balance required to ensure a secure and resilient digital environment.

The first pillar of the CIA Triad, confidentiality, deals with preventing unauthorized access to or disclosure of sensitive information. In a world where data breaches can lead to identity theft, financial fraud, and even national security risks, ensuring that only authorized individuals can access specific information is paramount. Encryption plays a pivotal role in upholding confidentiality. Encryption prevents unauthorized individuals from deciphering the information by converting data into an unreadable format, even if they manage to intercept it. Robust access controls, such as strong authentication mechanisms and role-based permissions, further bolster confidentiality by limiting access to authorized personnel only.

Integrity, the second facet of the CIA Triad, focuses on the accuracy and trustworthiness of data. It encompasses the prevention of unauthorized alterations, deletions, or modifications to information by malicious actors. Maintaining data integrity is critical in an era where misinformation can spread like wildfire and data manipulation can have far-reaching consequences. Hashing algorithms, which generate unique identifiers (hashes) for data sets, are fundamental to ensuring integrity. By comparing the hashes of the received data and the original data, organizations can identify any unauthorized changes. Additionally, digital signatures provide a means of verifying the authenticity of data and the identity of the sender, ensuring that data remains untampered throughout its journey.

Availability, the third pillar of the CIA Triad, ensures authorized users have timely and uninterrupted access to information and services. Critical systems and data availability are paramount in e-commerce, healthcare, or emergency services. Downtime can result in financial losses, disruption of services, and even endanger lives. Redundancy and fault tolerance mechanisms play a central role in maintaining availability. Organizations can mitigate the impact of hardware failures, cyber attacks, and natural disasters by employing backup systems, load balancing, and disaster recovery plans. The advent of cloud computing has further enabled high availability through distributed data centers and seamless failover mechanisms.

Confidentiality, Integrity, and Availability synergy create a delicate equilibrium, demanding thoughtful trade-offs and strategic decisions. Striking the right balance between these principles is essential. For instance, enhancing one aspect may inadvertently compromise another. A stringent access control mechanism that maximizes confidentiality may inadvertently hinder availability by causing delays in data access. Thus, cybersecurity professionals must navigate these intricate relationships to design comprehensive security architectures.

In the face of evolving cyber threats, the CIA Triad encounters challenges that demand continuous adaptation. As the digital landscape expands, ensuring confidentiality becomes more complex. Encryption standards evolve to withstand increasingly sophisticated attacks, and methods of securely managing encryption keys become critical. Ensuring integrity requires tackling issues such as insider threats and the rise of deepfake technology that can manipulate audio and video content. Availability, too, faces challenges in the form of distributed denial of service, or DDoS, attacks that overwhelm systems, requiring sophisticated traffic filtering mechanisms.

As technology evolves, the CIA Triad must evolve as well. The Internet of Things (IoT) introduces many interconnected devices, raising concerns about maintaining confidentiality and integrity while ensuring availability. Artificial intelligence and machine learning present both opportunities and challenges, as they can be used to enhance security measures but can also be leveraged by attackers to devise sophisticated attacks. Additionally, as data privacy regulations tighten globally, organizations must navigate the intricate compliance landscape, further influencing how the CIA Triad is implemented.

In the dynamic digital landscape, Confidentiality, Integrity, and Availability principles remain steadfast cornerstones of cybersecurity. The CIA Triad provides a robust framework for organizations to defend against cyber threats by safeguarding sensitive information, maintaining data accuracy, and ensuring uninterrupted access. As technologies evolve and new challenges emerge, the synergy of these principles will continue to shape the strategies and solutions employed to create a secure and resilient digital future. Cybersecurity professionals play a pivotal role in fortifying the digital realm against an ever-evolving array of threats by balancing the delicate interplay of confidentiality, integrity, and availability.

Principle of Least Privilege

In the intricate landscape of modern cybersecurity, where digital systems store a wealth of sensitive data and critical operations are conducted online, the Principle of Least Privilege (PoLP) emerges as a fundamental strategy to safeguard against breaches, data leaks, and unauthorized access. PoLP, which is based on the idea that individuals and entities should only be given the bare minimum of access, tries to minimize risks by lowering the attack surface and limiting the possible damage in the event of a breach. This section delves into the Principle of Least Privilege, exploring its core principles, practical applications, and the pivotal role it plays in constructing robust and resilient security architectures.

At its core, the Principle of Least Privilege embodies the idea of providing individuals and systems with the minimum level of access required to perform their specific tasks while denying unnecessary permissions. This concept applies across various levels of computing environments, from operating systems and applications to network access and data repositories. By adhering to PoLP, organizations ensure that no internal or external user has access beyond what is essential for their designated roles.

One of the primary benefits of PoLP is the reduction of the attack surface – the potential entry points that attackers can exploit to infiltrate systems or gain unauthorized access. When users are granted only the privileges necessary for their tasks, the avenues for attackers to exploit vulnerabilities are limited. For instance, an employee with administrative privileges on a company's server is a prime target for attackers. By employing PoLP, this user would have restricted access, minimizing the damage that can occur even if their credentials are compromised.

The real-world application of the Principle of Least Privilege encompasses multiple layers of access control. At the operating system level, user accounts are assigned specific roles, ensuring they can only interact with files, applications, and system settings relevant to their responsibilities. In network environments, firewalls and intrusion detection systems are configured to enforce access rules that align with PoLP. Application development is also crucial in PoLP; developers must design software that requests only the permissions necessary for its functionality rather than indiscriminately accessing user data.

The Principle of Least Privilege is difficult to put into practice. Balancing security and usability is a delicate task. Overzealous application of PoLP can lead to decreased productivity, as users may struggle to perform tasks that require slightly elevated privileges. Furthermore, the complexities of modern systems and interconnected networks can make it challenging to accurately define the "least privilege" for each user and application.

Role-Based Access Control (RBAC) is a robust implementation strategy for the Principle of Least Privilege. In RBAC, users are assigned to roles based on their job responsibilities, and permissions are granted at the role level rather than the individual user level. This approach simplifies access management by grouping users with similar needs and reducing the granularity of access control lists. RBAC enhances security by minimizing the chances of human error in assigning permissions and making managing access rights easier as users change roles within an organization.

The Principle of Least Privilege goes beyond human users to include processes and applications. Just as users should be granted the minimum necessary access, processes should also be confined to the required resources. Containerization and sandboxing are techniques used to isolate processes and applications, preventing them from accessing resources outside their designated environment. This enhances security by containing potential vulnerabilities and improves system stability and performance.

Incorporating the Principle of Least Privilege into an organization's culture requires a shift in mindset. Employees and users need to understand the rationale behind PoLP and how it contributes to overall security. Comprehensive training programs can educate staff about the risks of excessive privileges, the benefits of restricted access, and their role in upholding cybersecurity.

As technology evolves, the Principle of Least Privilege must adapt to new challenges. For example, cloud computing and remote work arrangements introduce access control complexities. Additionally, the expansion of Internet of Things (IoT) devices creates many potential entry points, demanding a reevaluation of access policies. Artificial intelligence and machine learning also offer opportunities to enhance access control through anomaly detection and behavior analysis.

The Principle of Least Privilege is a cornerstone of modern cybersecurity, offering a pragmatic approach to safeguarding digital assets and sensitive information. By reducing the attack surface, limiting the potential impact of breaches, and mitigating the risks associated with excessive access, PoLP creates a resilient foundation for secure computing environments. In an age where cyber threats and data breaches are constant concerns, organizations that embrace the Principle of Least Privilege demonstrate their commitment to proactive and effective cybersecurity practices. As technology advances, this principle remains a guiding light, illuminating the path to a safer digital future.

Defense-in-Depth Strategy

In an era where every keystroke, transaction, and communication traverses the intricate web of cyberspace, the need for comprehensive cybersecurity has become paramount. Enter the Defense-in-Depth strategy – a multifaceted approach emphasizing the significance of deploying multiple layers of security measures to safeguard against the diverse and ever-evolving landscape of cyber threats. This section delves into the Defense-in-Depth strategy, exploring its core principles, practical applications, and the critical role it plays in fortifying the digital realm against various potential attacks.

At its essence, the Defense-in-Depth strategy revolves around the notion that no single security measure can provide foolproof protection against the myriad of cyber threats. Organizations create a resilient and dynamic security ecosystem by implementing multiple layers of defense, each designed to mitigate specific risks. This approach acknowledges that attackers employ a variety of tactics to breach systems and that a comprehensive defense strategy must counteract these varied methods.

The Defense-in-Depth strategy encompasses a range of protective layers, each designed to address distinct facets of cybersecurity. These layers often include:

Perimeter Security: The outermost layer acts as a first line of defense, preventing unauthorized access to a network. Firewalls, intrusion detection systems, as well as intrusion prevention systems are pivotal in monitoring and filtering incoming traffic.

Network Security: Once within the network, attackers can exploit vulnerabilities. Network security measures, such as network segmentation, VLANs (Virtual LANs), and VPNs (Virtual Private Networks), compartmentalize resources to limit the lateral movement of attackers.

Endpoint Security: Endpoints have become prime targets for cyber attacks with the proliferation of connected devices. Endpoint security solutions safeguard individual devices, including antivirus software, anti-malware tools, and host-based intrusion detection systems.

Application Security: Insecure applications can provide gateways for attackers. Application security measures involve secure coding practices, regular updates, and vulnerability assessments.

Data Security: Protecting sensitive data is paramount. Encryption, tokenization, and data loss prevention tools ensure that even if data is breached, it remains unintelligible to unauthorized individuals.

Identity and Access Management (IAM): By controlling who has access to what, IAM systems ensure that only authorized individuals can access specific resources. Multi-factor authentication (MFA) as well as role-based access control (RBAC) are vital components.

Physical Security: The physical protection of infrastructure and hardware cannot be overlooked. Secure data centers, access controls, and video surveillance contribute to the overall security posture.

Security Awareness and Training: Human error is a significant factor in cyber breaches. Regular training and awareness programs help employees recognize phishing attempts, social engineering tactics, and other forms of cyber manipulation.

The strength of the Defense-in-Depth strategy lies in the synergy of its layers. Just as attackers might overcome one layer, they encounter another obstacle at the next level. For example, if a phishing email bypasses perimeter defenses, a vigilant employee trained in recognizing social engineering might thwart the attack. This approach ensures that even if one line of defense is breached, the attacker's progress is hindered, buying precious time for response and mitigation.

Implementing the Defense-in-Depth strategy demands a holistic approach considering an organization's unique architecture, risk profile, and resources. It requires a comprehensive assessment of assets, vulnerabilities, and potential threats. However, challenges include the complexity of managing multiple layers, the potential for overburdening systems with redundant security measures, and the cost of deploying and maintaining diverse solutions.

As cyber threats continue to develop, so must the Defense-in-Depth strategy. Emerging technologies, including Internet of Things (IoT) devices, cloud computing, and artificial intelligence introduce new attack vectors and challenges. Cloud security, for instance, involves collaboration between organizations and cloud providers to ensure data integrity and compliance. IoT devices, often with limited security features, can become entry points if not adequately protected. And while AI can enhance threat detection, attackers can also use it to devise sophisticated attacks.

While technology is pivotal in the Defense-in-Depth strategy, the human element remains crucial. A culture of cybersecurity awareness and vigilance is essential. Regular training, incident response drills, and a clear understanding of security policies empower employees to become the first line of defense against cyber threats.
In an era where the digital realm is both a boon and a battleground, the Defense-in-Depth strategy is a pillar of modern cybersecurity. By embracing the complexity of multiple layers, organizations create a resilient architecture capable of adapting to the ever-evolving threat landscape. While no strategy can provide absolute immunity against cyber attacks, the Defense-in-Depth approach acknowledges that organizations can safeguard their digital assets, information, and operations with a dynamic and layered defense by orchestrating a symphony of protective measures. As technology advances, the Defense-in-Depth strategy remains a

testament to the adaptability and innovation underpinning modern cybersecurity practices.

CHAPTER III

Building a Strong Foundation

Importance of Regular Software Updates and Patches

In the dynamic landscape of the digital age, where technology evolves at a staggering pace, the importance of regular software updates and patches cannot be overstated. From personal devices to critical infrastructure, software forms the foundation of our interconnected world. However, as software solutions become more intricate, so do the vulnerabilities malicious actors seek to exploit. This section delves into the critical significance of regular software updates and patches, exploring their role in enhancing cybersecurity, improving performance, and safeguarding against many potential threats.

Software vulnerabilities serve as entry points for cyber attackers seeking to infiltrate systems, steal sensitive data, and wreak havoc. These vulnerabilities often stem from coding errors, design flaws, or unforeseen interactions between software components. Armed with a deep understanding of these vulnerabilities, Hackers can exploit them to launch attacks ranging from data breaches to ransomware infections. Regular software updates and patches are the front lines of defense against these vulnerabilities. Developers continually analyze and test software to identify weaknesses, releasing updates that fix these issues and closing the doors that attackers seek to pry open.

As technology advances, so too does the attack surface available to cybercriminals. The Internet of Things (IoT) devices proliferation, mobile apps, and cloud-based solutions introduces a vast array of potential targets. With each new technology, hackers uncover novel methods of exploiting weaknesses, often at a speed that outpaces defensive efforts. Regular updates are essential to keep up with this rapidly shifting landscape. They enable developers to address emerging threats, enhance security mechanisms, and adapt to new attack vectors, ensuring that software remains resilient in the face of evolving risks.

Zero-day vulnerabilities, so named because developers have "zero days" to respond before an exploit is launched, underscore the urgency of software updates. Hackers often discover these vulnerabilities before developers, providing attackers with a window of opportunity to exploit systems before a patch is available. While organizations work diligently to uncover and address these vulnerabilities, regular software updates can significantly mitigate the impact of zero-day attacks. Even if an attacker discovers a zero-day vulnerability, a subsequent update can close the exploit, rendering the attack ineffective.

Regular software updates are central to the broader goal of building a resilient cybersecurity posture. Organizations can thwart common attack vectors such as malware infections, phishing attempts, and ransomware attacks by maintaining up-to-date software. Software updates usually entail security patches that address known vulnerabilities, rendering systems impervious to attacks that target these weak points. Neglecting updates, on the other hand, exposes systems to a higher risk of compromise, potentially leading to data breaches, financial losses, as well as reputational damage.

While cybersecurity is a primary motivation for software updates, performance optimization is an equally compelling reason. Software updates often include performance enhancements, bug fixes, and efficiency improvements. Developers identify and rectify bottlenecks, memory leaks, and other issues that can slow down systems as software evolves. This improves the end-user experience and extends the longevity of hardware by ensuring that software runs efficiently.

Regular software updates are vital to maintaining compliance in an era of growing data privacy regulations and industry standards. Regulatory bodies require organizations to adopt security measures that protect sensitive data and ensure that software remains current. Failing to comply to these regulations can lead to substantial fines and legal repercussions. Furthermore, as technologies advance and software becomes more integrated, updates often introduce compatibility improvements that ensure the software remains functional in an evolving ecosystem.

Despite the evident benefits of regular software updates, user resistance remains a challenge. Individuals often hesitate to update software due to concerns about disruptions, changes in user interface, or potential compatibility issues. However, organizations can counter this resistance by educating users about the importance of updates and highlighting their role in enhancing security and performance. User training programs emphasizing the risks of outdated software and the ease of updating can foster a culture of proactive cybersecurity.

While regular software updates are essential, there are challenges to navigate. Organizations must strike a balance between maintaining security and minimizing disruption. Updates that require system restarts or involve significant changes to functionality can impact productivity and user satisfaction. Therefore, careful planning, communication, and testing are critical to ensure a seamless update process.

The importance of frequent software updates and patches cannot be overlooked in a landscape defined by innovation and interconnectedness. Updates are the foundation of digital resilience, from shoring up vulnerabilities and mitigating risks to optimizing performance and staying compliant. By embracing a culture of proactive cybersecurity and recognizing the symbiotic relationship between software development and security, organizations can confidently navigate the ever-changing digital landscape. As technology advances and threats evolve, regular software updates are a testament to our ability to adapt, innovate, and safeguard the digital realm.

Secure Password Practices and Two-Factor Authentication

In the interconnected landscape of the digital age, where every aspect of life, from personal communication to financial transactions, occurs online, the importance of secure password practices and two-factor authentication (2FA) cannot be overstated. As technology evolves and cyber threats become increasingly sophisticated, the fundamental act of safeguarding digital identities through strong passwords and additional layers of authentication has become a critical component of modern cybersecurity. This section delves into the significance of secure password practices and two-factor authentication, exploring their role in defending against cyberattacks, mitigating the risks of data breaches, and empowering individuals to navigate the digital realm confidently.

Weak and easily guessable passwords are an open invitation to cyber attackers seeking unauthorized access to sensitive data and systems. Common passwords such as "123456" or "password" remain distressingly prevalent, providing attackers with a low-hanging fruit to compromise accounts. Moreover, with the advent of sophisticated password-cracking tools and techniques, attackers can swiftly breach accounts protected by weak passwords. Secure password practices serve as the first line of defense against these threats. Creating strong, complex passwords that combine uppercase and lowercase letters, numbers, and symbols significantly increases the difficulty of brute-force attacks and reduces the chances of unauthorized access.

Creating strong passwords entails a balance between complexity and length. A longer passphrase comprising a sequence of words or random characters is inherently more secure than a short, complicated password. Passphrases are not only easier to remember but also harder to crack, making them an excellent choice for securing accounts. For instance, "PurpleElephant$Balloons" is a robust passphrase that combines unrelated words and special characters. Employing such passphrases across various accounts ensures that even if one password is compromised, attackers cannot gain access to other accounts.

As online accounts grow, the challenge of managing strong passwords becomes daunting. This is where password managers shine. Password managers create and store complex passwords for various accounts, allowing users to access their credentials through a master password or biometric authentication. These tools not only enhance security by eliminating the need to remember numerous passwords but also reduce the likelihood of reusing passwords across different platforms, a practice that magnifies the impact of a data breach.

While secure password practices offer robust protection, they can be further fortified by implementing two-factor authentication (2FA) or multi-factor authentication (MFA). 2FA requires users to provide two verification forms before accessing an account: something they know (a password) and something they have (a physical device). This secondary layer of authentication significantly raises the bar for attackers, as even if they acquire a password, they would also need physical possession of a device, such as a smartphone, to complete the authentication process.

Two-factor authentication offers various methods for the second layer of authentication. One common approach is using a text message or an authentication app to receive a one-time code that must be entered alongside the password. Other methods include biometric authentication, such as fingerprints or facial recognition, and hardware tokens that generate time-based codes. The diversity of 2FA methods allows users to choose the one that aligns with their preferences and enhances their security posture.

Data breaches have become a pervasive concern, with even the most secure platforms falling victim to cyberattacks. In the aftermath of a breach, compromised passwords can be sold on the dark web, exposing individuals to identity theft and unauthorized account access. 2FA acts as a safeguard in such scenarios. Even if a password is compromised, the additional layer of authentication prevents attackers from gaining access without the second factor, rendering stolen credentials useless.

While 2FA offers robust protection, challenges remain in its adoption. Some users may find the additional step cumbersome or worry about the security of their second factor, such as a smartphone. Educating users about the benefits of 2FA and addressing their concerns is crucial to encourage widespread adoption. Many online platforms and services now offer 2FA as an optional feature, making it increasingly accessible to users seeking enhanced security.

Secure password practices and two-factor authentication reflect a broader cultural shift in cybersecurity. As individuals and organizations recognize the value of digital identities and the potential repercussions of compromised accounts, proactive measures become essential. Educating users about the risks of weak passwords and the benefits of 2FA fosters a culture of cyber awareness and responsibility. It empowers individuals to take charge of their digital security, reducing the overall risk landscape and creating a more resilient digital environment.

In the digital age, where the boundaries between the physical and virtual worlds blur, secure password practices and two-factor authentication stand as guardians of our digital identities. Individuals and organizations bolster their cybersecurity defenses by employing strong, complex passwords and embracing the added layer of authentication offered by 2FA. These practices not only thwart cyber attackers but also empower users to navigate the digital realm with confidence, secure in the knowledge that their data, accounts, and online interactions are safeguarded against an array of potential threats. As technology advances and threats evolve, the partnership between secure password practices and two-factor authentication remains a testament to our ability to innovate, adapt, and secure the digital frontier.

Employee Training and Awareness Programs

In the modern digital landscape, where technology permeates every facet of life, the human element remains a keystone in cybersecurity. Despite the proliferation of cutting-edge tools and technologies, the actions as well as the decisions of individuals within an organization can significantly impact its security posture. Employee training and awareness programs have emerged as crucial strategies to cultivate a vigilant and informed workforce, transforming employees into the first line of defense against cyber threats. This section delves into the significance of cybersecurity employee training and awareness programs, exploring their role in mitigating risks, fostering a culture of cyber resilience, and empowering individuals to navigate the digital realm confidently.

While technological advancements have revolutionized how organizations operate, they have also ushered in an era of unprecedented cyber risks. Malicious actors exploit the human element as a vector of attack, often using tactics such as phishing, social engineering, and spear phishing to manipulate employees into compromising security. Inadvertent actions like clicking on a malicious link or sharing sensitive information can lead to data breaches, financial losses, and reputational damage. Recognizing that technology alone cannot thwart these threats, organizations are turning to the human factor as a potent line of defense.

Employee training and awareness programs aim to educate staff about the intricacies of cyber threats, equip them with the knowledge to identify potential risks, and empower them to respond effectively. These programs cover various topics, including phishing awareness, password hygiene, safe browsing practices, and the secure use of company devices and networks. Organizations create a human firewall as a vital barrier against attacks by arming employees with these skills.

Human errors, frequently brought on by education or a lack of awareness can have major consequences. Misconfigured settings, improper handling of sensitive data, and falling for social engineering tactics are typical examples of such errors. Employee training programs address these pitfalls, providing individuals with the insights to make informed decisions. Through simulations, case studies, and interactive exercises, employees learn to recognize and avoid potential pitfalls, reducing the possibility of security breaches caused by human error.

Employee training and awareness programs contribute to cultivating an organization's cyber resilience culture. When individuals understand the importance of cybersecurity and their role in safeguarding digital assets, they become more proactive in detecting and reporting potential threats. This shift in mindset transforms employees from passive technology users into active participants in the organization's defense strategy. A culture of cyber resilience encourages continuous learning, adaptability, and a collective commitment to upholding security standards.

As the landscape of cyber threats evolves, so must employee training and awareness programs. Cyber attackers constantly refine their tactics, ensuring employees stay informed about the latest threat vectors and attack techniques. Programs should be updated regularly to address emerging threats and encompass a diverse range of scenarios to prepare employees for various situations. In addition to traditional classroom-style training, organizations incorporate gamification, simulations, and interactive modules to engage employees and enhance learning outcomes.

Effective cybersecurity is a collective effort that involves personnel from various departments, not just IT specialists. Employee training and awareness programs bridge the gap between IT and non-IT personnel, ensuring that individuals across the organization understand their role in maintaining a secure environment. Non-technical employees, such as human resources staff or marketing professionals, are provided with the knowledge and tools needed to contribute to the organization's cybersecurity objectives.
Implementing successful employee training and awareness programs is challenging. Resistance to change, employee turnover, and the dynamic nature of cyber threats can pose obstacles. To address these challenges, organizations should tailor their training programs to resonate with the workforce, highlight real-world examples of cyber incidents, and demonstrate the tangible benefits of cybersecurity awareness.
Additionally, creating a supportive environment where employees feel comfortable reporting potential threats without fear of repercussions is essential.

The digital landscape is marked by constant change, and employee training and awareness programs must reflect this reality. Organizations should emphasize continuous learning and provide resources for employees to stay updated about emerging threats, industry best practices, and new cybersecurity technologies. Regular refreshers and updates to training materials ensure that employees remain well-informed and capable of adapting to evolving threats.

In a world where digital interconnectedness accelerates the pace of innovation and risk alike, employee training and awareness programs are vital pillars of modern cybersecurity. By educating employees about cyber threats, instilling secure practices, and fostering a culture of vigilance, organizations create a human firewall that augments the capabilities of technological defenses. Empowered by knowledge and armed with the skills to detect and respond to threats, individuals become integral contributors to the organization's security posture. As technology advances and threats evolve, the partnership between cybersecurity professionals and educated employees will remain a steadfast foundation of cyber resilience in an ever-changing digital landscape.

CHAPTER IV

Network Security

Firewalls and Intrusion Detection Systems (IDS)

In the vast and intricate landscape of the digital realm, where information flows seamlessly across networks and systems, the need for robust security measures has never been more pronounced. As cyber threats evolve in sophistication and scope, organizations must deploy advanced tools to defend against many potential attacks. Firewalls and Intrusion Detection Systems (IDS) have emerged as fundamental components of modern cybersecurity strategies, forming a dynamic duo that fortifies digital frontiers, detects anomalous activities, and shields sensitive data from malicious intent. This section delves into the significance of firewalls and intrusion detection systems, exploring their functions, types, implementation strategies, and pivotal roles in creating a secure and resilient digital environment.

Cyber threats have become an omnipresent concern in a world driven by technology, where data is a currency and information is power. Malicious actors exploit vulnerabilities in networks and systems, seeking unauthorized access, data breaches, and disruption of critical services. In response, organizations deploy many security measures to safeguard their digital assets. The symbiotic partnership of firewalls and intrusion detection systems is at the forefront of this defense.

Firewalls serve as the digital gatekeepers that regulate traffic flow between networks. Much like their real-world counterparts, firewalls create a barrier that separates trusted internal networks from potentially hostile external networks, controlling the entry and exit of data packets. Firewalls operate at both the hardware and software levels and analyze incoming and outgoing traffic based on predefined rules. These rules can be configured to enable or deny access based on factors such as IP addresses, port numbers, and protocols. By enforcing these rules, firewalls prevent unauthorized access, mitigate the risk of malware infections, and thwart a wide array of cyber threats.

Firewalls come in various types, each tailored to address specific security requirements. Network firewalls, or packet-filtering firewalls, examine data packets as they traverse networks, making access decisions based on predetermined rules. These firewalls effectively prevent direct attacks from external sources but may not be sufficient to address sophisticated threats. On the other hand, application-layer firewalls operate at the application layer of the network stack, scrutinizing the content of data packets. This enables them to filter traffic based on specific applications, protocols, and user activities. Application-layer firewalls offer enhanced security by identifying and blocking more advanced threats, such as SQL injection attacks and cross-site scripting.

While firewalls establish the initial line of defense, intrusion detection systems play a complementary role by actively monitoring network and system activities for signs of suspicious behavior. IDS are designed to identify abnormal patterns and deviations from regular traffic, flagging potential security breaches for further investigation. Unlike firewalls, which primarily focus on preventing unauthorized access, IDS identifies ongoing or attempted attacks. They accomplish this through a combination of signature-based detection, which involves matching incoming data against known attack patterns, and anomaly-based detection, which identifies deviations from established baseline behavior.

Intrusion Detection Systems come in two primary forms: network-based IDS (NIDS) and host-based IDS (HIDS). NIDS monitors network traffic and analyzes data packets as they traverse the network infrastructure. They are particularly effective at detecting threats that target multiple systems, such as distributed denial of service (DDoS) attacks. HIDS, on the other hand, focuses on individual hosts or endpoints, monitoring activities within the operating system and applications. HIDS is adept at identifying unauthorized access attempts and potential malware infections. The synergy between NIDS and HIDS creates a multifaceted approach to intrusion detection, ensuring that potential threats are detected at both the network and host levels.

The collaboration between firewalls and intrusion detection systems resembles a well-choreographed dance. Firewalls establish access control rules that allow or deny traffic based on predefined criteria. On the other hand, IDS monitors these traffic patterns and activities for signs of unauthorized or suspicious behavior. When an IDS detects potentially malicious activity, it alerts security personnel or administrators. This prompts a response that could involve tightening firewall rules to block suspicious traffic or launching an investigation to ascertain the nature and scope of the threat. The harmonious interaction between firewalls and IDS enhances an organization's ability to thwart cyber threats effectively.

Implementing firewalls and intrusion detection systems requires a holistic strategy that aligns with an organization's risk profile and security objectives. For instance, in large networks, a combination of network- and application-level firewalls is advisable to provide comprehensive protection. Organizations may also employ intrusion prevention systems (IPS), an IDS extension. IPS detects threats and takes proactive measures to block or mitigate them in real-time.

The effectiveness of intrusion detection systems hinges on continuous monitoring and analysis of network and system activities. By establishing a baseline of normal behavior, IDS can accurately identify deviations that may signal an attack or intrusion attempt. Additionally, regular updates to IDS signature databases are essential to recognize new and emerging threats. These updates ensure that the system remains equipped to detect the latest attack patterns and tactics used by malicious actors.

While firewalls and IDS significantly bolster cybersecurity, challenges persist. False positives, where legitimate activities are flagged as suspicious, can lead to alert fatigue and reduced effectiveness. Balancing robust security and a streamlined workflow is essential. Additionally, the evolution of cyber threats demands that firewalls and IDS adapt and innovate. Machine learning and also artificial intelligence are being integrated into intrusion detection systems to enhance their ability to detect complex and evolving threats.

In a world where the digital landscape is teeming with opportunities and risks, firewalls and intrusion detection systems are guardians of digital boundaries. They create a protective barrier that mitigates unauthorized access, prevents cyber attacks, and ensures the integrity of data and systems. As technology advances and cyber threats grow in complexity, the partnership between firewalls and IDS remains essential in fortifying the digital frontier. By deploying these tools, organizations pave the way for a secure and resilient digital environment, where sensitive information, critical services, and digital interactions remain shielded from the ever-evolving landscape of cyber threats.

Virtual Private Networks (VPNs) for Secure Communication

In an era where digital communication forms the backbone of our personal and professional interactions, the need for secure and private data transmission has become paramount. Virtual Private Networks (VPNs) have emerged as a vital tool in the arsenal of cybersecurity measures, providing individuals and organizations with a secure pathway through the vast and often treacherous digital wilderness. This section delves into the significance of Virtual Private Networks, exploring their functions, benefits, types, implementation strategies, and their pivotal role in safeguarding digital communication and upholding privacy in an interconnected world.

The pervasive nature of digital communication presents an array of security challenges. When data traverses the open highways of the internet, it becomes susceptible to interception, surveillance, and unauthorized access. Public Wi-Fi networks, commonly used for convenience, lack the encryption necessary to protect sensitive information from prying eyes. Cyber attackers, equipped with sophisticated tools and techniques, exploit these vulnerabilities to launch attacks ranging from eavesdropping to data theft. Secure data transmission has become a fundamental requirement in a world where information holds immeasurable value.

Virtual Private Networks offer a compelling solution to digital communication's security concerns. A VPN establishes a secure, encrypted tunnel between the user's device and a remote server. This tunnel encapsulates the data in a protective layer, shielding it from potential attackers and unauthorized observers. The encrypted pathway ensures that even if intercepted, the data remains unintelligible, maintaining the confidentiality and integrity of the communication.

At the core of a VPN's functionality lies encryption, which transforms plain text data into a jumbled, unreadable format. This encryption, typically achieved through protocols like OpenVPN, IPSec, or L2TP/IPSec, is the armor that guards against interception. Alongside encryption, VPNs utilize tunneling protocols to encapsulate the encrypted data in packets, creating a secure conduit for communication. By routing traffic through this tunnel to a remote server, VPNs mask the user's true IP address, enhancing anonymity and preventing potential attackers from tracing the communication back to its origin.

The benefits of Virtual Private Networks extend beyond security to encompass enhanced online privacy. As users' data is routed through a remote server, their true IP addresses are replaced with the server's IP. This not only cloaks their digital footprint but also circumvents geo-restrictions and censorship imposed by governments or institutions. Individuals can access content that may be regionally restricted, while organizations can communicate freely across borders, unencumbered by location-based limitations.

Virtual Private Networks come in various configurations, tailored to the needs of individuals and organizations. Remote Access VPNs provide secure connections for individual users, enabling them to access a private network remotely. This is particularly useful for remote workers needing to access company resources securely. On the other hand, site-to-site VPNs establish encrypted connections between different networks, often across different physical locations. Organizations employ this type of VPN to establish secure communication between their various branches or offices.

Implementing a VPN strategy involves selecting the appropriate approach that aligns with an individual's or organization's security requirements. One common approach is to use a commercial VPN service, which offers a user-friendly interface and a wide range of server locations. However, this approach entails trusting the VPN service provider, as they can access the user's data. For those seeking greater control, setting up a self-hosted VPN using open-source software is an option. This allows users to manage their servers and control their data entirely.

Although VPNs have several advantages, they cannot solve every problem associated with digital security challenges. Users should be aware of potential limitations, such as reduced connection speeds due to the encryption and tunneling processes. Additionally, the effectiveness of a VPN depends on the provider's commitment to privacy and security. Users must research and select reputable VPN service providers that adhere to strict no-logs policies and utilize robust encryption protocols.

As technology evolves, so do VPNs. While they have traditionally been associated with privacy and security, VPNs are increasingly used for diverse purposes. Some organizations use VPNs to establish secure connections for IoT devices, ensuring that data transmitted between devices and servers remains protected. Additionally, as the prevalence of remote work continues to grow, VPNs have become a critical tool for maintaining secure connections between remote workers and corporate networks.

As technology develops and the digital environment evolves, the significance of secure and private communication remains steadfast. The Internet of Things (IoT) devices proliferation, smart cities, and interconnected systems underscores the need for comprehensive privacy solutions. With their ability to establish secure connections and shield data from interception, VPNs are poised to play a central role in preserving privacy in this rapidly evolving environment. As technology advances and threats evolve, the evolution of VPNs will continue, offering individuals and organizations a reliable conduit for secure communication in an interconnected world.

In a world where data flows freely across networks, communication spans continents in an instant, and digital interactions are interwoven into the fabric of daily life, Virtual Private Networks stand as sentinels of privacy and security. By creating encrypted tunnels, masking IP addresses, and thwarting potential attackers, VPNs empower individuals and organizations to navigate the digital realm with confidence. They offer protection against cyber threats and the freedom to access information, communicate, and collaborate without fear of interception or surveillance. As technology develops and the digital environment evolves, VPNs remain a steadfast guardian, forging a path to digital privacy in an interconnected world.

Securing Wi-Fi Networks and Bluetooth Connections

In an era of seamless connectivity, Wi-Fi networks and Bluetooth connections have become indispensable conduits for communication, collaboration, and information sharing. Yet, the very convenience that defines these wireless technologies also exposes them to various security risks. Securing Wi-Fi networks and Bluetooth connections has become paramount as cyber threats grow in complexity and frequency. This section delves into the significance of wireless security, exploring strategies to safeguard Wi-Fi networks and Bluetooth connections, their vulnerabilities, and their role in ensuring privacy and data integrity in an interconnected world.

The proliferation of wireless technologies has revolutionized how we communicate and interact with digital devices. Wi-Fi networks enable us to access the internet from virtually anywhere, while Bluetooth connections facilitate seamless data exchange between devices nearby. However, the very attributes that make these technologies convenient – their accessibility and ubiquity – also make them susceptible to various security risks.

Wi-Fi networks, the backbone of modern digital communication, require robust security measures to defend against various threats. Unsecured or inadequately secured Wi-Fi networks are vulnerable to eavesdropping, unauthorized access, and data breaches. Hackers can intercept sensitive information, launch man-in-the-middle attacks, and compromise devices connected to the network. Organizations and individuals must implement comprehensive security protocols encompassing encryption, authentication mechanisms, and access controls to address these vulnerabilities.

Encryption is a fundamental pillar of Wi-Fi network security. Implementing encryption protocols, such as WPA2 (Wi-Fi Protected Access 2) or its successor, WPA3, safeguards data transmission by rendering intercepted information unintelligible to unauthorized individuals. Encryption ensures that even if an attacker obtain an access to the network, the data they intercept remains unreadable. It is imperative to use robust encryption protocols and avoid default or weak passwords to prevent attackers from deciphering encrypted data through brute-force attacks.

Authentication mechanisms are critical components of securing Wi-Fi networks. These mechanisms verify the identity of devices attempting to connect to the network, impeding unauthorized access. Strong authentication requires using complex, unique passwords and implementing multi-factor authentication (MFA) when possible. Enterprises often use enterprise-grade security measures, such as 802.1X authentication, which demands users to provide credentials before gaining network access.
Access controls dictate who can connect to a Wi-Fi network and what resources they can access. Employing robust access controls reduces the attack surface by limiting entry points for potential attackers. Network administrators can configure routers to use MAC (Media Access Control) filtering, allowing only devices with specific MAC addresses to join the network. While this is not foolproof, blocking devices with unauthorized MAC addresses adds an extra layer of defense.

Bluetooth technology, designed for short-range wireless communication, is commonly utilized for connecting devices like smartphones, headphones, and IoT devices. While Bluetooth connections offer convenience, they also introduce security vulnerabilities. Attackers can exploit Bluetooth vulnerabilities to gain unauthorized access, execute remote code execution, and intercept sensitive data. Understanding and reducing these risks is crucial to secure Bluetooth connections.

Bluetooth pairing is the procedure of establishing a secure connection between devices. There are two main types of Bluetooth pairing: Just Works and Numeric Comparison. Just Works is convenient but less secure, while Numeric Comparison involves users verifying a numerical code on both devices to ensure a secure connection. Choosing the more secure option helps mitigate the risk of unauthorized pairing.

Bluetooth devices are often set to "discoverable" mode to facilitate connections. However, this practice can expose devices to potential attackers in the vicinity. To reduce the risk of unauthorized connections, it is advisable to keep devices in non-discoverable mode when not actively establishing connections. This simple step limits the exposure of devices to potential attackers seeking vulnerable targets.

Like any technology, Bluetooth is not immune to vulnerabilities. Manufacturers periodically release security updates to address these vulnerabilities and enhance Bluetooth security. It is essential to keep devices and their associated software up to date to benefit from the latest security patches and improvements.

Effective wireless security strategies extend beyond technical measures. Raising users' awareness of the risks of unsecured Wi-Fi networks and Bluetooth connections is pivotal. Users should be knowledgeable about the importance of using strong, unique passwords, enabling encryption, and being cautious when connecting to public Wi-Fi networks. A well-informed user is better equipped to make security-conscious decisions and contribute to the overall security posture.

Wi-Fi networks and Bluetooth connections have transformed how we communicate and interact with technology. However, their ubiquity also exposes them to a myriad of security risks. Securing Wi-Fi networks and Bluetooth connections is not a one-size-fits-all endeavor. It requires a combination of encryption, authentication, access controls, and user awareness to create a robust defense against evolving cyber threats.

As technology develops and the digital environment evolves, the importance of wireless security remains steadfast. Organizations and individuals must remain vigilant, adapt to new attack vectors, and implement best practices to safeguard their networks and devices. By building strong digital foundations through secure Wi-Fi networks and Bluetooth connections, we can confidently navigate the wireless landscape, ensuring that our data, privacy, and digital interactions remain shielded from the ever-evolving realm of cyber threats.

CHAPTER V

Data Protection and Encryption

Data Encryption Methods and Algorithms

In an era where data is not only a valuable asset but also a vulnerable target, the importance of encryption cannot be overstated. Encryption is a potent tool to protect sensitive information from prying eyes, ensuring its confidentiality and integrity even in the face of sophisticated cyber threats. As technology advances, encryption methods and algorithms are pivotal in creating secure digital environments. This section explores the significance of data encryption, delving into various encryption methods, cryptographic algorithms, their applications, and their dynamic role in cybersecurity.

In a digitally interconnected world, where information flows freely across networks and systems, the potential for unauthorized access, interception, and data breaches is ever-present. Data encryption addresses these concerns by transforming plain text information into a ciphered form, rendering it unreadable without the appropriate decryption key. This process provides a vital layer of protection, whether the data is at rest within storage systems or in transit across networks. Encryption ensures that even if an attacker obtain an access to the data, they cannot decipher its contents without the necessary decryption key.

Symmetric encryption, also known as secret-key encryption, forms the foundation of secure communication. In this method, a single secret key is used both for encryption and decryption. The sender utilizes this key to encrypt the data before transmission, and the recipient uses the same key to decrypt the data upon receipt. While symmetric encryption offers efficiency and speed, the challenge lies in securely sharing the secret key between parties. Any compromise of the key would result in the exposure of the encrypted data. To mitigate this risk, methods like the Diffie-Hellman key exchange are employed to exchange symmetric encryption keys over insecure communication channels securely.

By using a pair of keys—a public key for encryption along with a private key for decryption—asymmetric encryption, also known as public-key encryption, presents a revolutionary method of encryption. These keys are mathematically related but computationally infeasible to derive one from the other. The sender employs the recipient's public key to encrypt the data; only the recipient possessing the corresponding private key can decrypt it. Asymmetric encryption addresses the key distribution challenge of symmetric encryption, as the public keys can be freely shared while the private keys remain closely guarded. This method also enables digital signatures, ensuring data integrity and authenticating the sender.

Numerous cryptographic algorithms underpin data encryption methods, each designed to provide specific security properties. The Advanced Encryption Standard (AES), a symmetric-key algorithm, is widely used for encrypting data at rest and during transmission. It offers high security and efficiency, making it suitable for various applications. The RSA algorithm is renowned for facilitating secure communication, digital signatures, and key exchange on the asymmetric encryption front. RSA's strength lies in the mathematical complexity of factoring large prime numbers, which is the foundation of its security.

While encryption protects data confidentiality, hashing algorithms address data integrity and verification. Hash functions convert input data into fixed-length strings of characters, known as hash values or digests. Even a slight change in the input data results in a drastically different hash value. Hashing is used to verify data integrity, as any tampering or corruption would lead to a mismatch between the original and recalculated hash. Common hashing algorithms include SHA-256 (Secure Hash Algorithm 256-bit) and MD5 (Message Digest Algorithm 5).

Encryption application spans various sectors, from finance and healthcare to communication and government. In the financial industry, encryption safeguards sensitive financial transactions, protecting customers' financial data and ensuring compliance with regulatory requirements. In healthcare, encryption secures electronic health records, maintaining patient privacy and meeting Health Insurance Portability and Accountability Act (HIPAA) standards. Additionally, encryption plays a vital role in secure communication channels, online shopping, and protecting confidential government communications.

As technology advances, the landscape of data encryption faces a paradigm shift with the emergence of quantum computing. Traditional encryption methods, especially those reliant on factoring large prime numbers like RSA, are vulnerable to quantum attacks. Quantum computers have the ability to efficiently solve problems that are computationally infeasible for classical computers, threatening the security of current encryption methods. To counter this, researchers are exploring quantum-resistant cryptographic algorithms, designed to endure attacks from quantum computers.

An often-overlooked aspect of encryption is key management and lifecycle. The secure generation, storage, distribution, rotation, and destruction of encryption keys are essential to maintaining the overall security of encrypted data. Encryption keys should be protected from unauthorized access, ensuring that only authorized person can access them. Key management solutions and practices are vital to maintaining the confidentiality and integrity of encryption keys throughout their lifecycle.

Data encryption methods and algorithms are pioneers of digital trust in an era where privacy, security, and integrity are paramount. They empower individuals, organizations, and governments to communicate, collaborate, and transact confidently, knowing that their sensitive information is shielded from the reach of cyber attackers. Whether through symmetric or asymmetric encryption, hashing algorithms, or quantum-resistant cryptography, the principles of encryption ensure that the digital landscape remains a realm of possibilities rather than vulnerabilities. As technology evolves and threats advance, the evolution of encryption methods and algorithms will continue to pave the way for secure, resilient, and trustworthy digital environments.

Securing Data at Rest and in Transit

In the digital age, where data is the lifeblood of organizations and individuals alike, the imperative of data security has never been more pronounced. Data, whether at rest within storage systems or in transit across networks, is vulnerable to many threats ranging from cyberattacks to unauthorized access. Securing data at rest and in transit is a comprehensive approach that tackle the full spectrum of data protection, ensuring confidentiality, integrity, and availability. This section delves into the significance of securing data in both states, exploring strategies, technologies, and best practices to fortify data against the evolving landscape of cyber threats.

Data at rest refers to information stored in databases, servers, and other storage systems when it is not actively being used or transmitted. Despite its seemingly static state, data at rest is far from immune to security risks. Unauthorized access, insider threats, and physical theft can compromise sensitive data and have far-reaching consequences. A multi-faceted approach to securing data at rest is essential to mitigate these risks.

Encryption is a cornerstone of securing data at rest. It involves converting plaintext data into ciphertext through the use of cryptographic algorithms. Even if an attacker gains access to the encrypted data, they cannot decipher it without the appropriate decryption key. Various encryption methods, such as full-disk encryption (FDE), encrypting file systems, and database encryption, provide protection against unauthorized access to stored data. FDE ensures that all data on a storage device is encrypted, making it unreadable to anyone without the decryption key.

Effective encryption requires robust key management practices. Encryption keys are essential for both encrypting and decrypting data. Properly managing these keys is crucial to maintaining the security of encrypted data. Keys should be generated securely, stored in a protected environment, rotated periodically, and audited regularly. By implementing a comprehensive key management strategy, organizations can hinder unauthorized access to sensitive data and maintain control over encryption processes.

Securing data at rest also involves its proper disposal when it is no longer needed. Data retention policies and practices ensure that data is retained for the required period and then securely deleted. Secure data destruction methods, such as cryptographic erasure or physical destruction of storage media, prevent residual data from being recovered by malicious actors. Proper disposal of data-bearing devices, such as hard drives and smartphones, is essential to eliminate the risk of data breaches stemming from discarded devices.

Data in transit refers to information that is moving from one location to another over a network. Whether it's sending an email, conducting online transactions, or accessing cloud services, data in transit traverses various network nodes and can be intercepted by attackers. Safeguarding data in transit is vital to prevent unauthorized access, eavesdropping, and data manipulation during transmission.

Transport Layer Security (also known as TLS) and its predecessor, Secure Sockets Layer (SSL also known as), are cryptographic protocols designed to secure data in transit. TLS/SSL encrypts the communication channel between two devices, ensuring that data exchanged remains confidential and cannot be intercepted by unauthorized entities. It is commonly used to secure web communications, online banking, and email transmissions.

Virtual Private Networks (VPNs) establish encrypted tunnels for data transmission over public networks. A VPN routes data through a remote server, encrypting it along the way. This shields data from potential attackers and provides a further layer of security for users accessing the internet from untrusted networks. VPNs are commonly used by remote workers, travelers, and individuals seeking to enhance their privacy online.

Application layer security mechanisms, such as digital signatures and message authentication codes (MACs), protect data integrity during transmission. Digital signatures provide a means of verifying the sender's authenticity and ensuring that the data has not been tampered with. MACs use cryptographic algorithms to generate a unique code accompanying the data, allowing the recipient to verify its integrity upon receipt.

In the era of cloud computing, data in transit often traverses complex, distributed environments. Cloud service providers typically offer built-in encryption and security features to safeguard data during transmission. However, it remains essential for users to understand the security measures in place and implement additional encryption methods if required, especially when dealing with sensitive or regulated data.

While securing data in transit is essential, it is important to balance security and performance. The encryption and decryption processes can introduce latency, impacting data transmission speed. Organizations must carefully select encryption algorithms and parameters to ensure data remains secure without compromising performance.

Securing data at rest and in transit is not a one-size-fits-all endeavor but requires a comprehensive and multi-layered approach. By encrypting data at rest, implementing strong key management practices, and securely disposing of data, organizations ensure that stored information remains confidential and immune to unauthorized access. Meanwhile, securing data in transit through encryption protocols like TLS/SSL and VPNs ensures that data exchanges occur in a protected environment. In an ever-evolving landscape of cyber threats, a holistic approach to data security – encompassing both data at rest and in transit – is essential to safeguarding digital assets, preserving privacy, and maintaining the integrity of information in an interconnected world.

Managing Encryption Keys

In data security, encryption stands as a stalwart guardian, protecting sensitive information from the prying eyes of cyber adversaries. At the heart of encryption's efficacy lies the management of encryption keys – the digital gatekeepers that unlock the hidden treasures of encrypted data. As organizations increasingly rely on encryption to safeguard their digital assets, managing encryption keys emerges as a critical discipline. This section delves into the significance of encryption key management, exploring its principles, challenges, best practices, and its pivotal role in upholding encrypted information's confidentiality, integrity, and availability.

Encryption keys are the linchpin of data security. They are the cryptographic codes that govern the transformation of plaintext data into unreadable ciphertext and vice versa. Encryption converts data into an incomprehensible format without the appropriate key, ensuring that even if an unauthorized entity obtain an access to the encrypted data, it cannot decipher its contents. Encryption key management encompasses these keys' generation, distribution, storage, rotation, and destruction throughout their lifecycle. It ensures that the keys remain securely stored and accessible only to authorized parties.

The process of encryption begins with the generation of encryption keys. These keys are mathematically derived and hold the power to both lock and unlock encrypted data. Key generation involves using strong random number generators or cryptographic algorithms to create statistically improbable keys to be replicated or guessed. The quality of key generation directly impacts the security of the encrypted data; weak keys are susceptible to brute-force attacks and compromise the very essence of encryption.

Once generated, encryption keys must be securely distributed to authorized parties. Key distribution poses a challenge, especially in environments where geographical distribution and diverse devices are commonplace. Secure channels, such as encrypted communications and secure couriers, ensure that keys reach their intended recipients without interception by malicious actors. In some cases, asymmetric encryption is employed to securely exchange symmetric encryption keys, further enhancing key distribution security.

The secure storage of encryption keys is pivotal to data security. Keys stored in an accessible or unprotected manner are an open invitation to potential attackers. Hardware Security Modules (HSMs), specialized devices designed for key management and cryptographic operations, provide a secure environment for key storage. HSMs are tamper-resistant, offering protection against physical attacks and unauthorized access attempts. Additionally, key management solutions with robust access controls restrict key retrieval and usage to authorized personnel.

Encryption keys, like any security measure, have a finite lifespan. Regular key rotation is essential to minimize the risk of a compromised key leading to prolonged data exposure. Key rotation involves generating new keys and gradually transitioning encrypted data from the old key to the new one. While key rotation introduces complexity, it is a proactive measure that mitigates the impact of a potential key compromise. The frequency of key rotation depends on the organization's risk profile and the encrypted data's criticality.

In situations where keys are compromised, lost, or no longer needed, proper key revocation and destruction are vital. Revocation involves invalidating a compromised or outdated key to prevent its future use. Destruction ensures a key is rendered irretrievable, minimizing the risk of unauthorized decryption. Secure key destruction methods involve cryptographic erasure, rendering the key's binary representation irrecoverable.

Managing encryption keys is challenging. The intricacy of key management increases with the scale of data and the number of keys involved. Balancing security and usability can be tricky – overly stringent key management practices can hinder operational efficiency, while lax practices compromise security. Additionally, key escrow, where a third party holds a copy of the encryption key, raises concerns about data privacy and trust. Balancing security, usability, and compliance remains a constant challenge for organizations.

Effective encryption key management requires adherence to best practices that align with an organization's security objectives. Centralizing key management through dedicated solutions like Key Management as a Service (KMaaS) streamlines the management process and provides a holistic view of key lifecycles. Regular auditing and monitoring of key usage and access logs help detect any anomalies or unauthorized activities. Implementing multi-factor authentication and role-based access controls ensures only authorized personnel can access and manage keys.

In an era where data breaches and cyberattacks dominate headlines, encryption key management emerges as the unsung hero safeguarding digital fortresses. The effectiveness of encryption hinges on the security of its keys – the secrets that enable data to be securely hidden and revealed. Through the meticulous processes of key generation, distribution, storage, rotation, and destruction, encryption key management upholds the core principles of data security: confidentiality, integrity, and availability. As organizations navigate the complexities of the digital landscape, the guardianship of encryption keys remains paramount – an enduring commitment to protect the secrets that shield the digital treasures of the modern world.

CHAPTER VI

Web Security

Safe Browsing Practices

The importance of safe browsing practices cannot be overstated in the vast landscape of the internet, where information flows freely and opportunities abound. While offering immense benefits, the digital realm also presents a variety of security risks that can compromise personal privacy, sensitive data, and even financial well-being. Safe browsing practices serve as a shield against cyber threats, empowering individuals to explore the online world with confidence while minimizing the risk of falling victim to cyberattacks. This section delves into the significance of safe browsing practices, exploring strategies to enhance online security, techniques to identify and avoid potential threats, and the role these practices play in preserving the integrity of the digital experience.

The digital landscape is replete with cyber threats that target individuals, businesses, and organizations. Malware, phishing attacks, malicious websites, and social engineering are just a few examples of the threats that users encounter while browsing the internet. Malware, including viruses, ransomware, and spyware, can infect devices and steal sensitive information. Phishing attacks trick users into revealing personal information by posing as legitimate entities. Malicious websites host harmful content that can compromise devices and steal data.

Social engineering exploits psychological manipulation to deceive users into revealing confidential information or performing harmful actions.

Safe browsing practices are a proactive defense against the myriad online cyber threats. By adopting these practices, users can significantly reduce their vulnerability to attacks and protect their digital identities. Safe browsing practices encompass a range of techniques, from using secure connections and verifying website authenticity to employing strong authentication methods and staying vigilant against social engineering tactics. These practices are not limited to a single approach; they create a comprehensive strategy that mitigates risks across various online activities.

A fundamental safe browsing practice is ensuring secure connections while interacting with websites. Hypertext Transfer Protocol Secure (HTTPS) encrypts the data exchanged between a user's browser and a website's server, ensuring that sensitive information stays confidential and protected from eavesdropping. Secure connections are particularly crucial when sharing personal or financial information, such as during online transactions or when logging into accounts. Users should be cautious of websites without HTTPS, as they can expose their data to interception.

Before interacting with a website, it is essential to verify its authenticity to avoid falling victim to phishing attacks. Cybercriminals often generate fake websites that mimic legitimate ones to trick users into revealing sensitive information. Users should carefully examine the website's domain, check for misspellings or variations, and look for security indicators like the padlock icon and HTTPS in the address bar. Additionally, avoiding clicking on links from unsolicited emails or messages helps prevent inadvertently landing on malicious websites.

Employing strong authentication methods is a key aspect of safe browsing practices. Multi-factor authentication (MFA) adds a further layer of security by requiring users to provide multiple verification forms before accessing an account. This can entail something the user knows (password), something the user has (a smartphone for receiving a verification code), and something the user is (biometric authentication like fingerprints or facial recognition). MFA significantly minimizes the risk of unauthorized access, even if a password is compromised. Social engineering tactics prey on human psychology and trust to manipulate users into revealing sensitive information or performing actions that compromising security. Safe browsing practices include maintaining a healthy skepticism when encountering unsolicited personal or financial information requests. Users should be cautious of requests for passwords, financial details, or login credentials via email or messages. Verifying the sender's authenticity through a separate communication channel can prevent falling victim to these deceptive tactics.

Regularly updating software, operating systems, and applications is a crucial safe browsing practice. Software updates often entail security patches that address vulnerabilities that attackers can exploit. Neglecting updates leaves devices susceptible to known exploits that cybercriminals can leverage. Users should enable automatic updates whenever possible and regularly check for updates to make sure they are using the latest, most secure software versions.

In an age where the digital realm is woven into the fabric of daily life, safe browsing practices are the compass that guides users through the intricacies of the internet while protecting them from its potential pitfalls. By adopting secure connections, verifying website authenticity, embracing strong authentication, and remaining vigilant against social engineering tactics, individuals can fortify their online experience. Safe browsing practices empower users to confidently explore, transact, and communicate in the digital world, knowing they are equipped with the knowledge and tools to navigate the digital landscape safely. As technology advances and cyber threats evolve, the commitment to safe browsing practices remains essential in preserving the integrity of personal information and ensuring a secure and enjoyable online experience.

Avoiding Phishing and Social Engineering Attacks

The threat of phishing as well as social engineering attacks looms large in the vast expanse of the digital world, where connectivity and communication thrive. These cunning tactics prey on human psychology, exploiting trust, curiosity, and urgency to deceive individuals into divulging sensitive information, clicking malicious links, or performing harmful actions. As cybercriminals continue to evolve their techniques, it becomes imperative for individuals and organizations to arm themselves with knowledge and strategies to thwart these insidious attacks. This section delves into the intricacies of phishing and social engineering attacks, exploring their mechanisms, identifying red flags, and delving into robust strategies to build digital resilience against these threats.

Phishing attacks and social engineering are tactics that exploit human behavior rather than solely relying on technical vulnerabilities. Phishing attacks typically involve sending deceptive emails that mimic legitimate communications from trusted entities, such as banks, online services, or coworkers. These emails carry malicious links or attachments that, when interacted with, can lead to data breaches, malware infections, or unauthorized access. Social engineering encompasses a broader range of techniques that manipulate human psychology, often involving tactics like pretexting, baiting, tailgating, or quid pro quo to extract information or gain access.

Recognizing the red flags of phishing and social engineering attacks is paramount to avoiding falling victim to these tactics. Emails that exhibit urgency, such as demanding immediate action or threatening consequences, often indicate phishing attempts. Poor grammar, misspellings, and generic greetings can also indicate a malicious email. Additionally, requests for sensitive information like passwords, financial details, or Social Security numbers should raise suspicion, especially when communicated via email or messages.

Verifying the sender's authenticity is a crucial step in avoiding phishing attacks. Rather than clicking on links provided in emails, users should manually type in the website's URL to ensure they are visiting a legitimate site. Hovering over links to reveal the actual URL before clicking can also help identify suspicious links. Contacting the purported sender through a separate communication channel, such as a known phone number, can confirm the legitimacy of the communication.

Attachments and email links are common vehicles for delivering malware or redirecting users to malicious websites. Users should exercise caution before opening attachments or clicking links, even if the email appears to be from a trusted source. Hovering over links to preview the URL, avoiding shortened URLs, and using browser extensions that expand short URLs can provide insights into the link's destination.

In social engineering attacks, education emerges as a powerful defense. Organizations should conduct regular awareness training sessions to educate employees about the tactics employed by cybercriminals. Training should cover the importance of strong passwords, recognizing suspicious emails, and adhering to security policies. Creating a culture of skepticism and vigilance can significantly reduce the success rate of social engineering attacks.

Implementing multi-factor authentication (MFA) is a robust defense against unauthorized access, especially in social engineering attacks. MFA requires users to provide multiple verification forms before accessing an account or system. This can entail something the user knows (password), something the user has (a smartphone for receiving a verification code), and something the user is (biometric authentication like fingerprints or facial recognition). Even if an attacker gains access to a password, MFA serves as a second line of defense. Creating channels for users to report suspicious activities or emails is essential for a proactive defense against phishing and social engineering attacks. Organizations should establish clear reporting procedures and encourage users to report any emails or interactions that raise suspicion. This facilitates swift action, allowing security teams to investigate and take necessary measures to prevent further attacks.

In an era of unprecedented connectivity and reliance on digital interactions, the threat of phishing and social engineering attacks remains a formidable challenge. By understanding the mechanisms of these attacks, recognizing red flags, and adopting proactive strategies, individuals and organizations can build digital resilience against the tactics of cyber adversaries. Safe email practices, vigilant scrutiny of attachments and links, and adopting multi-factor authentication are effective shields against the evolving landscape of cyber threats. As technology advances and cybercriminals refine their techniques, the commitment to building digital resilience becomes essential to preserving the integrity of personal and organizational information. Through knowledge, awareness, and collective vigilance, individuals and organizations can confidently navigate the digital world, knowing they are equipped to recognize and thwart the artful manipulations of phishing and social engineering attacks.

Secure Development Practices for Websites and Web Applications

In the era of digitalization, where websites and web applications serve as gateways to the online world, the significance of secure development practices cannot be overstated. As the digital landscape expands, so does the threat surface for cyberattacks. Malicious actors target vulnerabilities in websites and web applications to steal data, compromise systems, and wreak havoc. Secure development practices are the bedrock of creating resilient and trustworthy online platforms that safeguard user data, maintain data integrity, and mitigate the risk of cyber threats. This section delves into the importance of secure development practices for websites and web applications, exploring strategies, techniques, and best practices to foster a culture of security in the development process.

Websites and web applications are dynamic ecosystems interacting with users and processing sensitive data. The architecture of these digital platforms introduces vulnerabilities that attackers can exploit to compromise security. Cross-Site Scripting, Cross-Site Request Forgery, SQL injection, and insecure authentication are just a few of the vulnerabilities that can be exploited if not addressed during the development phase. These vulnerabilities enable attackers to execute malicious scripts, steal data, gain unauthorized access, and manipulate user interactions.

Secure development practices entail integrating security considerations into every software development life cycle phase. From the initial design and coding to testing and deployment, security must be a constant companion. This approach, known as Secure Software Development Life Cycle (SDLC), emphasizes that security is not an afterthought but an integral part of the development process. Secure SDLC incorporates threat modeling, code reviews, vulnerability assessments, and security testing to identify and rectify vulnerabilities before they are exploited.

Threat modeling is a proactive approach to determine potential vulnerabilities and attack vectors early in development. By analyzing the architecture, data flow, and interactions of a website or application, developers can anticipate how attackers might exploit weaknesses. Threat modeling empowers development teams to prioritize security measures and allocate resources effectively, ensuring critical vulnerabilities are addressed before deployment.

Secure coding practices lie at the core of building secure websites and web applications. Developers should adhere to coding standards and guidelines that mitigate common vulnerabilities. Input validation and output encoding prevent injection attacks, such as SQL injection and XSS. Employing prepared statements for database queries and parameterized queries prevents data manipulation vulnerabilities. Regularly updating libraries and components, which may contain known vulnerabilities, is another crucial aspect of secure coding.

Authentication and authorization mechanisms are pivotal in ensuring that users have appropriate access to resources. Strong authentication practices, including password hashing and salting, prevent unauthorized access to user accounts. Implementing role-based access control ensures that users are granted permissions based on their roles and responsibilities. By adhering to the principle of least privilege, developers can mitigate the risk of attackers gaining excessive access rights.

Injection attacks, like SQL injection and also Cross-Site Scripting (XSS), exploit data input and output vulnerabilities. By implementing strict input validation, developers can ensure that only expected data formats are accepted, preventing malicious code from being injected. Output encoding involves transforming data into a safe format to display in a web browser, mitigating the risk of malicious scripts executing in users' browsers. Security testing is an essential component of secure development practices. Regular security testing, including dynamic application security testing (DAST) and static application security testing (SAST), helps uncover vulnerabilities that might have been overlooked during development. DAST involves testing the application in a running state to identify potential vulnerabilities, while SAST examines the source code for weaknesses.

Secure development practices extend beyond the deployment phase. Continuous monitoring and incident response protocols ensure that websites and web applications are regularly assessed for vulnerabilities and anomalies. Monitoring traffic patterns, user interactions, and system performance can help detect unauthorized activities and potential breaches. Having incident response plans enables swift action in case of a security incident, minimizing the impact on users and data.

In an era where digital interactions shape personal and professional lives, the security of websites and web applications is a shared responsibility. Secure development practices are the linchpin that fortifies the digital landscape against cyber threats. Developers create platforms that users can trust by embedding security from inception, adhering to secure coding practices, implementing robust authentication and authorization mechanisms, and embracing regular security testing. Secure development practices pave the way for a digital frontier where data integrity, user privacy, and system resilience are paramount. As technology develops and cyber threats become more sophisticated, the commitment to secure development practices remains a beacon of trust in the ever-changing digital world.

CHAPTER VII

Mobile Device Security

Securing Smartphones and Tablets

In an era of digital mobility, smartphones and tablets have become essential companions, offering convenience, connectivity, and a gateway to a myriad of online experiences. However, as these devices seamlessly integrate into every facet of our lives, their security implications cannot be overlooked. Smartphones and tablets store personal data, connect to various networks, and access sensitive applications, making them prime cyberattack targets. Securing these devices goes beyond safeguarding data – it ensures the protection of privacy, the integrity of communications, and the prevention of unauthorized access. This section delves into the critical importance of securing smartphones and tablets, exploring strategies, best practices, and technologies that empower users to embrace digital mobility confidently.

Smartphones and tablets have transcended their role as communication tools to become integral to modern life. These devices store a treasure trove of personal information, including emails, contacts, photos, financial data, and sensitive applications. This wealth of data makes them appealing targets for cybercriminals seeking to exploit vulnerabilities for financial gain, identity theft, or unauthorized access. Moreover, the ever-expanding app ecosystem introduces potential vectors for malware and unauthorized data access.

Device security serves as the foundation for securing smartphones and tablets. Strong device security measures mitigate the risk of unauthorized access and data breaches. This begins with setting up strong PINs, passwords, or biometric authentication methods like fingerprints or facial recognition. Enabling device encryption ensures that data stored on the device is inaccessible without the proper credentials, even if the device falls into the wrong hands.

Regularly updating smartphones and tablets' operating system (OS) is paramount to maintaining security. OS updates often include patches for known vulnerabilities and security enhancements. Failing to update exposes devices to known exploits that attackers can leverage. Enabling automatic updates ensures that devices have the latest security fixes, effectively closing the vulnerability window.

The app ecosystem enriches the capabilities of smartphones and tablets, but it also introduces potential security risks. Users must exercise caution when downloading apps and only use official app stores, like the Apple App Store or Google Play Store. Reading app reviews, checking app permissions, and avoiding apps that request excessive permissions can prevent inadvertently granting access to sensitive data or compromising device security.

Securing network connections is crucial to preventing unauthorized access and data interception. Users should connect to trusted and secure Wi-Fi networks, avoiding open or unsecured networks that expose data to eavesdropping. When connecting to public Wi-Fi, using a Virtual Private Network (VPN) encrypts internet traffic, providing an additional layer of security against potential attackers.

For organizations, mobile device management (MDM) solutions provide a centralized approach to securing smartphones and tablets used by employees. MDM enables organizations to enforce security policies, remotely manage devices, and guarantee compliance with security standards. This is particularly important for maintaining data security in a corporate environment where sensitive information is accessed and shared on mobile devices.

Biometric authentication methods, such as fingerprints and facial recognition, balance convenience and security. These methods provide a seamless and user-friendly way to unlock devices and authenticate users. However, it's essential to understand that biometric data is sensitive and must be securely stored and transmitted to prevent unauthorized access.

Mobile antivirus and security apps offer an additional layer of defense against malware and cyber threats. These apps scan devices for malicious software, provide real-time protection, and offer anti-phishing features that warn users about potentially harmful websites or links. While such apps can enhance device security, users should ensure they are reputable and regularly updated.

If a smartphone or tablet is lost or stolen, remote wiping and tracking capabilities can prevent unauthorized access to sensitive data. Enabling these features allows users to erase device data and track the device's location remotely. These features provide a last line of defense to protect data and mitigate the potential impact of device loss.

Securing smartphones and tablets is not merely a technical endeavor; it's a commitment to safeguarding personal privacy, digital identity, and the integrity of communications. As these devices become extensions of ourselves, their security becomes paramount. By implementing strong device security, regularly updating operating systems, scrutinizing app permissions, securing network connections, and considering biometric authentication, users can navigate the realm of digital mobility with resilience. Organizations can leverage mobile device management solutions to ensure corporate data security. In the digital age, where connectivity knows no bounds, securing smartphones and tablets empowers users to embrace the benefits of digital mobility while maintaining control over their digital lives. As technology advances and cyber threats evolve, the commitment to mobile security remains an enduring shield against the ever-changing landscape of digital risks.

Mobile App Security and Permissions

In the modern digital era, where smartphones have become extensions of our lives, mobile apps are integral in providing convenience, entertainment, and utility. However, with this convenience comes the responsibility of safeguarding sensitive data and user privacy. Mobile app security and permissions are at the forefront of ensuring that users' personal information remains confidential and their digital experiences remain free from cyber threats. This section delves into the realm of mobile app security, exploring the importance of permissions, the risks associated with data access, and strategies to empower users to make informed decisions while maintaining control over their digital identities.

Mobile app security encompasses the practices, measures, and technologies put in place to protect the app itself and the data it interacts with. As the demand for apps grows, so does the need to ensure that they are developed and maintained with security in mind. Mobile apps can act as gateways to personal information, ranging from contact details and location to financial and even biometric information. Failing to secure these apps exposes users to various threats, including data breaches, unauthorized access, and identity theft.

Permissions form the cornerstone of mobile app security, defining what information an app can access and utilize. When users install an app, they often grant permissions that allow the app to access specific parts of their device, such as the camera, microphone, location, contacts, and more. While these permissions enable apps to provide enhanced functionality, they also introduce potential risks if misused or exploited.

Users must understand the permissions they grant to apps and the implications of these permissions. The first step towards mobile app security is ensuring that users are informed about the data access that an app requires. App stores typically display a list of permissions an app requests before installation. Users should review these permissions and consider whether they align with the app's intended functionality. For instance, a weather app requesting contact access may raise concerns and warrant further investigation.

Over-permissioned apps, or apps that request excessive permissions unrelated to their core functionality, pose significant security risks. These apps may collect sensitive data without the user's knowledge or consent, leading to potential privacy breaches. Malicious actors can exploit over-permissioned apps to access personal data, which can be used for various purposes, including identity theft, fraud, or even blackmail.

While many apps require specific permissions to function properly, balancing app functionality and user privacy is crucial. Users should be cautious when granting permissions unrelated to the app's core features. For instance, a photo editing app should not need access to a user's location data. Reading user reviews and researching the app's reputation can provide insights into how it handles user data.

Modern operating systems offer users greater control over app permissions. Users can grant or revoke specific permissions for installed apps, allowing for a more granular approach to data access. Users can revoke permission to limit potential risks if an app no longer requires specific permission for its intended use. Regularly reviewing and adjusting app permissions helps maintain control over data access.

Choosing reputable app stores is integral to mobile app security. Official app stores, which include the Apple App Store and Google Play Store, vet apps before making them available to users. These stores have security mechanisms to identify and remove malicious or deceptive apps. Sideloading apps from third-party sources can introduce significant security risks, as these apps may not undergo the same level of scrutiny. Regularly updating apps ensures users benefit from security patches that address known vulnerabilities. Developers continually refine apps to enhance security and performance. Outdated apps may contain security flaws that attackers can exploit. Enabling automatic app updates can streamline the process and ensure that apps are always up-to-date.

As mobile apps continue to shape how we communicate, work, and entertain ourselves, the focus on mobile app security becomes paramount. Users can confidently navigate the app ecosystem by understanding app permissions, making informed decisions about data access, and regularly reviewing and adjusting permissions. App developers play a vital role in building secure apps that respect user privacy and adhere to best practices in data handling. App stores, as gatekeepers, contribute to the security landscape by vetting apps and removing those that pose risks. In a digital age where data is both precious and vulnerable, mobile app security is not merely a technical endeavor – it's a commitment to protecting digital identities and fostering a secure and trustworthy app ecosystem. As technology advances and new threats emerge, the vigilance towards mobile app security remains essential to preserving the integrity of personal information and the continuity of a secure digital experience.

Mobile Device Management (MDM) Solutions

In the dynamic landscape of the digital age, where smartphones and tablets have become indispensable tools for personal and professional tasks, the need for effective mobile device management (MDM) solutions has never been more pronounced. Mobile devices are no longer merely for communication; they are gateways to sensitive data, critical applications, and organizational networks. MDM solutions offer a centralized approach to managing and securing these devices, ensuring data privacy, enforcing security policies, and maintaining the integrity of corporate assets. This section explores the significance of MDM solutions, their role in enhancing mobile security, and the strategies they offer to navigate the complexities of the mobile era.

MDM solutions are comprehensive frameworks that allow organizations to manage and monitor mobile devices from a centralized platform. From enforcing security policies and configuring device settings to remotely deploying applications and ensuring compliance, MDM solutions provide organizations with the tools needed to manage the myriad challenges a mobile workforce presents effectively. With employees using diverse devices across different locations, MDM solutions bridge the gap between productivity and security.

As mobile devices have become essential in both personal and professional contexts, they have also emerged as prime targets for cyberattacks. Mobile malware, data breaches, and unauthorized access pose significant threats, requiring organizations to adopt proactive security measures. MDM solutions mitigate these risks by offering a unified approach to device security, data protection, and user access control.

One of the primary functions of MDM solutions is enforcing security policies across a range of mobile devices. Organizations can define policies that dictate device-level settings, such as passcode requirements, encryption standards, and biometric authentication. These policies create a standardized security baseline that helps prevent unauthorized access and mitigate potential risks from lost or stolen devices.

The ability to manage devices remotely is a hallmark feature of MDM solutions. In the event of a lost or stolen device, administrators can remotely lock, locate, or wipe the device to hinder unauthorized access to sensitive data. This capability safeguards organizational information and reduces the risk of data breaches resulting from compromised devices.

MDM solutions streamline the deployment and management of applications across various devices. Organizations can remotely distribute applications to employees, ensuring they have access to the tools needed to perform their tasks effectively. Furthermore, MDM solutions enable administrators to control app permissions, update schedules, and ensure compliance with licensing agreements.

MDM solutions enable organizations to implement user access controls that balance convenience and security. Through identity and access management (IAM) integration, administrators can ensure that only the authorized users can access sensitive applications and data. Multi-factor authentication (MFA) can be enforced, adding an extra layer of security beyond traditional passwords.

The Bring Your Own Device (also known as BYOD) trend has gained prominence, allowing employees to use their personal devices for work tasks. While BYOD can enhance flexibility and productivity, it also introduces security challenges. MDM solutions offer mechanisms to compartmentalize work and personal data on the same device, ensuring that organizational data remains isolated and protected.

In today's regulatory landscape, organizations are held to rigorous data protection and privacy standards. MDM solutions provide the means to enforce security policies that align with industry regulations and standards. Additionally, these solutions offer reporting capabilities that allow organizations to demonstrate compliance efforts and respond promptly to audits.

While MDM solutions offer substantial benefits, their implementation can pose challenges. Balancing security and user experience is paramount; overly restrictive policies can impede productivity, while lax policies can compromise security. Furthermore, the diversity of devices, operating systems, and user preferences demands a robust and adaptable MDM solution capable of addressing the complexities of a heterogeneous mobile environment.

In an age characterized by digital mobility, where the boundaries between personal and professional use of mobile devices blur, MDM solutions emerge as critical assets in an organization's security arsenal. These solutions offer a centralized approach to mobile device management, providing comprehensive security policies, remote management capabilities, application deployment, and access controls. By enabling organizations to navigate the complex terrain of mobile security, MDM solutions empower the workforce to confidently embrace digital mobility, knowing that their devices are secure and their sensitive data is protected. As technology evolves and mobile threats become more sophisticated, MDM solutions are guardians of the mobile landscape, ensuring that organizations can reap the benefits of mobile productivity while maintaining control over their digital assets.

CHAPTER VIII

Cloud Security

Benefits and Risks of Cloud Computing

In modern technology, cloud computing has emerged as a transformative force, reshaping how organizations and individuals manage, store, and access data and applications. With the promise of scalability, cost efficiency, and flexibility, cloud computing has become an integral component of digital transformation strategies across industries. However, as with any technological advancement, cloud computing presents a dual nature, carrying both substantial benefits and inherent risks. This section delves into the world of cloud computing, exploring its advantages and the potential pitfalls that organizations and users must navigate as they ascend into the digital sky.

One of the most well-known benefits of cloud computing is its scalability. Cloud platforms offer the ability to scale resources up or down based on demand. This dynamic scalability ensures that organizations can adjust their computing power, storage, and resources to match their needs, allowing for optimal performance during peak times and cost savings during quieter periods.

Cloud computing offers cost benefits by eliminating the need for organizations to invest heavily in hardware and infrastructure. With cloud providers handling the maintenance, updates, and hardware costs, organizations can adopt a pay-as-you-go model, paying only for the resources they consume. For startups and small enterprises, this shift from capital expenditure to operational expenditure is especially beneficial.

Users can access data and applications using cloud computing from anywhere with an internet connection, transcending geographical boundaries. This global accessibility promotes remote work, enhances collaboration among geographically dispersed teams, and facilitates real-time information sharing, thereby boosting productivity and efficiency.

Cloud service providers regularly update and maintain their infrastructure, ensuring users can access the latest features, security patches, and enhancements. This relieves organizations from managing and maintaining their IT infrastructure, enabling them to focus on core business operations.

Strong business continuity and disaster recovery solutions are provided by cloud computing. Data loss caused by hardware malfunctions, natural disasters, or other unforeseen events is less likely when data is kept in the cloud because it is simple to back up and replicate data across numerous locations.

One of the most well-known disadvantages of cloud computing is security and privacy concerns. Storing data in the cloud uncovers it to potential security breaches and unauthorized access. Organizations often entrust sensitive and confidential data to cloud providers, raising concerns about data security, encryption practices, and the risk of data leaks. Additionally, the location of data centers and compliance with data protection regulations may pose challenges to maintaining user privacy.

Organizations that rely heavily on cloud services may become dependent on their chosen service provider. This dependence can lead to vendor lock-in, making it challenging to switch providers or migrate data and applications back to on-premises environments if needed.

Cloud outages can disrupt operations, impacting user access to applications and data. While reputable cloud providers implement redundancy and failover mechanisms, downtime remains a risk, especially in instances of large-scale outages or technical glitches.

Uploading and downloading significant amounts of data to and from the cloud can result in significant bandwidth costs. Organizations must carefully consider the cost implications of data transfer, especially if they frequently move large datasets between their premises and the cloud.

Organizations relinquish a degree of control over their data and infrastructure when they migrate to the cloud. Cloud providers manage the underlying infrastructure, and changes in service terms, policies, or even service discontinuation can impact how organizations operate.

Organizations must conduct thorough due diligence when selecting a cloud service provider to mitigate risks and maximize benefits in cloud computing. This includes assessing the provider's security practices, compliance with data protection regulations, and reputation within the industry.

Implementing robust data encryption techniques can safeguard sensitive information from unauthorized access and breaches. Encryption should be employed both during data transmission and while data is at rest in the cloud.

Organizations can adopt hybrid or multi-cloud strategies to mitigate the risks of vendor lock-in and enhance reliability. These approaches involve using multiple cloud providers or a combination of cloud and on-premises solutions, offering greater flexibility and control.

Organizations should regularly monitor their cloud environment for security breaches and compliance violations. Implementing intrusion detection systems, firewalls, and security information and event management (SIEM) solutions can enhance threat detection and incident response capabilities.
A well-defined disaster recovery as well as business continuity plan is crucial for addressing potential cloud outages or data breaches. Organizations should establish protocols for data recovery, system restoration, and communication during disruptions.

Cloud computing has undeniably reshaped the digital landscape, offering unparalleled scalability, cost efficiency, and accessibility. However, the journey into the cloud has its challenges. The benefits of cloud computing must be weighed against the potential risks, including security concerns, vendor dependence, and data privacy issues. By implementing proactive security measures, conducting thorough research, and adopting strategies to mitigate risks, organizations can confidently harness the advantages of cloud computing while navigating the intricate cloudscape. As technology continues to evolve, the embrace of cloud computing signifies a technological shift and a strategic move towards reimagining how organizations leverage digital resources to achieve their goals in an ever-changing digital frontier.

Securing Data in the Cloud

The apperance of cloud computing has ushered in a new era of data storage and management, promising unprecedented scalability, accessibility, and cost efficiency. In this digital paradigm, where organizations and individuals entrust their most sensitive information to cloud service providers, the imperative of securing data in the cloud takes center stage. As data breaches, cyber threats, and privacy concerns continue to make headlines, the challenge lies in striking a delicate balance between harnessing cloud technology's benefits and safeguarding stored data's integrity and confidentiality. This section delves into the intricate landscape of securing data in the cloud, exploring strategies, technologies, and best practices that underpin trust and protection in the digital sky.

The dynamic nature of cloud computing introduces both unique opportunities and challenges to data security. Once confined to local servers and infrastructure, data is now dispersed across geographically diverse data centers managed by cloud providers. As organizations embrace this distributed model, the primary concern becomes ensuring that data remains confidential, available, and unaltered. The cloud's data security foundation rests on a multifaceted approach encompassing encryption, access controls, authentication mechanisms, regular monitoring, and proactive threat detection.

Encryption stands as a cornerstone of data security in the cloud. By converting data into an unreadable format using cryptographic algorithms, encryption ensures that even if unauthorized entities gain access to the data, they cannot decipher its contents. The cloud offers two primary forms of encryption: encryption at rest and encryption in transit.

Encryption at rest safeguards data stored in cloud servers, ensuring that it remains protected even when not in active use. Encryption in transit encrypts data as it travels between a user's device and the cloud, safeguarding against interception and eavesdropping.

Effective access controls and authentication mechanisms are paramount in securing data in the cloud. Multi-factor authentication (MFA), requiring users to provide two or more verification forms, adds layer of security beyond traditional passwords. Role-based access control (RBAC) assigns specific privileges based on user roles, preventing unauthorized access to sensitive information. Organizations can enforce least privilege principles, ensuring that users only have access to the data necessary for their roles, reducing the attack surface.

Selecting a trustworthy cloud service provider is a critical step in securing data in the cloud. Organizations should assess the provider's security practices, compliance certifications, and data protection mechanisms. Reputable providers adhere to industry standards and regulations, such as ISO 27001, SOC 2, and GDPR. Thoroughly understanding the provider's security responsibilities and establishing a clear demarcation between provider and user responsibilities is essential in establishing a strong security foundation.

Data loss prevention (DLP) solutions are pivotal in monitoring and preventing the unauthorized transmission of sensitive information. These solutions can detect and block attempts to transfer confidential data outside the organization's network, whether inadvertently or maliciously. Monitoring tools provide real-time insights into user activities, network traffic, and data access patterns. Regularly reviewing these logs and alerts enables organizations to promptly identify potential anomalies or unauthorized activities.

Data loss because of system failures, natural disasters, or cyberattacks is a constant threat in the digital realm. Implementing robust backup and disaster recovery plans is imperative for securing data in the cloud. Regularly backing up data and applications to geographically diverse locations ensures that data can be restored in the event of a loss. These measures safeguard business continuity and offer a way to recover from unexpected data breaches.

End-to-end encryption provides a futher layer of security by ensuring that data remains encrypted throughout its entire lifecycle, from creation to storage and transmission. This approach prevents cloud service providers from accessing the data in its readable form, thus enhancing data privacy. Effective key management is essential to control access to encryption keys, which are the keys to unlocking encrypted data. Organizations must carefully manage and safeguard encryption keys to prevent unauthorized access and data breaches.
While cloud computing offers convenience, organizations should consider data portability and lock-in mitigation strategies. Data portability allows organizations to move their data seamlessly between different cloud providers or back to on-premises infrastructure. This reduces the risk of vendor lock-in, enabling organizations to maintain control over their data and infrastructure choices. Securing

data in the cloud is not a singular action but a comprehensive strategy encompassing encryption, access controls, monitoring, disaster recovery, and prudent vendor selection. As cloud computing continues to shape the digital landscape, the challenges and

opportunities associated with data security persist. Organizations must recognize that securing data in the cloud is a shared responsibility between users and cloud service providers. By adopting a proactive as well as holistic approach to data security, organizations can confidently navigate the digital sky, harnessing the power of the cloud while safeguarding the lifeline of their digital operations. As technology evolves and the threat landscape continues to change, the commitment to securing data in the cloud remains an enduring
commitment to trust, privacy, and the resilience of the digital age.

Shared Responsibility Model with Cloud Providers

Cloud computing has transformed how organizations manage and process their data, offering unprecedented scalability, flexibility, and cost-efficiency. As businesses relocate their operations to the cloud, a pivotal concept known as the shared responsibility model emerges as a guiding principle for maintaining robust security in this dynamic landscape. This model outlines the distribution of security responsibilities between cloud service providers and their customers, emphasizing the collaborative effort required to ensure data protection and privacy. This section delves into the intricacies of the shared responsibility model, highlighting its significance, clarifying the roles of both providers and customers, and underscoring its role in forging a secure digital alliance.

The shared responsibility model forms the cloud's security foundation, outlining the distinct roles and obligations of both cloud service providers (CSPs) and their customers. In this alliance, CSPs assume responsibility for securing the underlying infrastructure, network, and physical facilities hosting the cloud services. Conversely, customers are tasked with securing their data, applications, operating systems, and configurations within the cloud environment.

Cloud service providers are responsible for safeguarding the foundational elements of the cloud ecosystem. This encompasses the physical security of data centers, the maintenance of hardware and networking components, and the implementation of security measures to hinder unauthorized access to their infrastructure. Providers also manage the virtualization layer, hypervisors, and host operating systems, ensuring their security and resilience. Leading cloud providers implement a plethora of security measures to fortify their infrastructure. These measures include robust firewalls, intrusion detection systems, and distributed denial-of-service (DDoS) protection. Regular security audits, vulnerability assessments, and also penetration testing bolster the provider's capacity to identify and address potential weaknesses, thus ensuring a strong defensive stance against cyber threats.
While cloud providers establish a secure foundation, customers actively secure their data, applications, and configurations within the cloud environment. Customers maintain the autonomy to configure security settings, implement access controls, and deploy encryption mechanisms to protect their assets from unauthorized access or data breaches. Properly configuring these settings is crucial, as improper configurations can lead to security vulnerabilities.

Customers must adhere to industry best practices and regulatory requirements when configuring their cloud environment. This involves configuring firewall rules, establishing strong authentication mechanisms, and defining access controls to ensure only authorized personnel can access critical resources. Regular security assessments as well as audits should be conducted to identify vulnerabilities, assess risks, and remediate potential weaknesses.

The shared responsibility model is more than a distribution of duties; it embodies a collaborative synergy between cloud providers and customers. Providers offer the tools, infrastructure, and expertise to create a secure foundation, while customers contribute by implementing security measures that align with their specific needs and risk profile. This cooperative approach harnesses the strengths of both parties to create a unified front against the evolving landscape of cyber threats.

Embracing the shared responsibility model empowers organizations to maintain control over their data and security posture. Customers can tailor security measures to their unique requirements, ensuring that sensitive data remains protected and compliance requirements are met. This model also enables organizations to adapt to changing security landscapes, seamlessly integrating new security tools and practices as threats evolve.
While the shared responsibility model is a robust framework, potential challenges exist. Misunderstandings or misconceptions about the division of responsibilities can lead to security gaps. Organizations must thoroughly comprehend the model and the specific obligations of both parties to ensure that security measures are correctly implemented.

Education is paramount in the shared responsibility model. Cloud providers should transparently communicate their security measures, the division of responsibilities, and the tools available to customers.

Customers, in turn, should educate their staff about best practices and security configurations to mitigate risks.

In the landscape of cloud computing, the shared responsibility model emerges as a beacon of security, uniting cloud service providers and customers in a common cause: protecting data and applications from the ever-evolving realm of cyber threats. By clarifying both parties' roles, obligations, and strengths, this model promotes collaboration, education, and empowerment. Cloud computing's transformative potential is fully realized when the shared responsibility model is embraced, forging a secure digital alliance that paves the way for innovation, growth, and a resilient defense against the challenges of the digital age. As technology advances and threats evolve, the shared responsibility model remains a dynamic framework that adapts and thrives, ensuring that security remains a cornerstone of the cloud ecosystem.

CHAPTER IX

Identity and Access Management

Role of IAM in Cybersecurity

In the intricate landscape of modern cybersecurity, where threats are pervasive and data is the currency of the digital realm, Identity and Access Management (IAM) emerges as a pivotal stronghold. IAM, the practice of managing and controlling user identities and their access to resources, plays a central role in fortifying an organization's digital defenses. IAM is more than a technological tool; it's a comprehensive strategy that safeguards sensitive information, ensures compliance, and empowers organizations to navigate the complex balance between accessibility and security. This section delves into the multifaceted role of IAM in cybersecurity, unraveling its significance, functions, challenges, and the evolving landscape in which it operates.

IAM serves as the linchpin of cybersecurity, addressing the fundamental principle that access to digital assets should be granted to authorized individuals and entities while preventing unauthorized access. As organizations embrace digital transformation, IAM becomes a critical enabler, offering a systematic approach to managing user identities, roles, and permissions across complex digital ecosystems. From mitigating the risk of data breaches to streamlining user access, IAM weaves a protective fabric that defends against the relentless tide of cyber threats.

IAM's core lies identity management, where users are uniquely identified and authenticated. Robust authentication mechanisms, like multi-factor authentication (MFA), bolster the traditional username-password combination, requiring users to provide multiple verification forms. This guarantees that only authorized personnel gain access, reducing the risk of unauthorized infiltration.

IAM encompasses the orchestration of access rights and permissions, ensuring that users are granted access only to resources that align with their roles and responsibilities. Role-based access control (also known as RBAC) and attribute-based access control (also known as ABAC) enable organizations to granularly define access privileges, reducing the attack surface and safeguarding sensitive information from unauthorized exposure.

Single Sign-On (SSO) is a pivotal component of IAM that empowers users to access multiple applications using a single set of credentials. SSO enhances user convenience and simplifies identity management, as users are managed from a centralized location. This consolidation reduces the need for users to remember multiple credentials, reducing the risk of password-related security breaches.

In an era of stringent data protection regulations like GDPR and HIPAA, IAM plays a crucial role in ensuring compliance. Organizations are mandated to protect sensitive user data, and IAM provides the mechanisms to control who can access this data and how it's used. Implementing proper IAM practices assists organizations in meeting regulatory requirements and avoiding potential penalties.

Despite its immense benefits, IAM has challenges. Ensuring a seamless user experience while maintaining stringent security can be a delicate balance. Complex infrastructures, diverse user roles, and evolving technology landscapes can complicate IAM implementations. As organizations transition to cloud environments and embrace remote work, IAM must adapt to ensure secure access from various locations and devices.

IAM is evolving to meet the demands of the modern digital landscape. Adaptive IAM, driven by artificial intelligence and machine learning, assesses user behaviors and risk profiles to determine appropriate access levels. This approach offers real-time adjustments to access privileges, enhancing security by responding to changes in user behavior or potential threats.

As organizations migrate to cloud environments, vendor Identity and Access Management (vIAM) solutions gain prominence. These solutions enable organizations to leverage the IAM expertise of cloud providers, reducing the burden of managing complex IAM systems. However, organizations must carefully evaluate vIAM offerings to ensure they align with their security and compliance requirements.

In the ever-evolving cybersecurity landscape, IAM is the sentinel of digital trust, overseeing the access points to valuable digital assets. Its multifaceted functions, from identity authentication to access management, contribute to safeguarding sensitive information, maintaining compliance, and establishing a secure digital environment. As organizations continue to grapple with a changing threat landscape, IAM evolves as a dynamic force, adapting to new challenges and technological advancements. In a world where the battle for digital security rages on, IAM remains an unwavering guardian, upholding the principles of accessibility, accountability, and protection in the digital age.

Single Sign-On (SSO) Solutions

In the intricate realm of digital interactions, where individuals traverse a multitude of applications and platforms, the need for efficient and secure access management has become paramount. Single Sign-On (SSO) solutions have emerged as a transformative force, streamlining user access to multiple applications while bolstering cybersecurity measures. SSO simplifies the authentication process, allowing users to log in once and gain access to various systems without repeatedly entering credentials. Beyond convenience, SSO solutions offer enhanced security, improved user experiences, and simplified identity management. This section delves into the world of Single Sign-On solutions, exploring their significance, mechanisms, benefits, challenges, and the evolving landscape in which they operate.

In an era where users interact with various applications spanning work, personal, and online services, SSO solutions address the challenge of managing numerous credentials. With the average person juggling multiple passwords, the risk of weak or reused passwords increases, posing a significant security threat. SSO alleviates this burden by offering a centralized authentication mechanism that grants access to various applications, reducing the need for users to remember and enter multiple sets of credentials.

SSO solutions operate through a federated authentication model. The SSO solution serves as an intermediary, easing the authentication process when a user tries to gain access to an application. The user's identity is verified upon initial login, and a unique token is generated. Subsequent requests to access other applications are validated using this token, negating the need for users to re-enter credentials. Using standards like the Security Assertion Markup Language (SAML) or OpenID Connect (OIDC) ensures interoperability between applications and SSO systems.

At the forefront of SSO solutions lie convenience and efficiency. Users experience streamlined access to various applications, enhancing productivity and user satisfaction. Moreover, SSO significantly reduces the likelihood of password-related security breaches, as users are not prompted to create and remember multiple passwords. This strengthens the overall security posture and minimizes the risk of unauthorized access resulting from weak or compromised credentials.

SSO solutions offer centralized control over user access, enabling administrators to enforce strong authentication measures. Multi-factor authentication (MFA) can be implemented at the SSO level, requiring users to provide additional verification forms beyond their passwords. This added layer of security fortifies the authentication process and mitigates the risk of unauthorized access.

SSO solutions simplify identity management by centralizing user authentication and access control. When a user changes roles or leaves an organization, administrators can easily revoke or modify access privileges across multiple applications from a single point. This ensures that access rights remain up-to-date and aligned with an individual's current responsibilities.

While SSO solutions offer numerous benefits, they are not immune to challenges. Implementing SSO requires careful planning, integration, and user education. The risk of a single point of failure is a concern; if the SSO solution experiences downtime, users may be locked out of all applications. Additionally, user privacy concerns may arise, as SSO solutions can access a broad range of user interactions across multiple platforms.

The landscape of SSO is evolving to address emerging challenges and enhance user experiences. Contextual SSO considers the user's context and location to determine the appropriate level of authentication required. For instance, if a user attempts to access sensitive data from an unfamiliar location, the SSO solution might prompt for additional authentication. Adaptive SSO leverages machine learning and behavioral analytics to assess user behavior and risk, dynamically adjusting the authentication process based on risk levels. In the digital age, where the boundaries between personal and professional interactions blur, Single Sign-On solutions emerge as the gateway to seamless and secure access. These solutions alleviate the burden of password management, enhance cybersecurity, and simplify identity management for organizations and users alike. As technology advances and threat landscapes evolve, SSO solutions continue to adapt, offering contextual and adaptive authentication mechanisms to meet the demands of a dynamic digital environment. By harnessing the power of SSO, organizations empower their workforce with the tools to navigate the digital landscape with confidence, productivity, and a heightened sense of security.

Multi-Factor Authentication (MFA) Implementation

In the ever-evolving realm of cybersecurity, where threats loom large and data breaches have become all too common, robust authentication measures have become paramount. Multi-Factor Authentication, or MFA, also known as Two-Factor Authentication (2FA) or Two-Step Verification, has emerged as a potent weapon in the arsenal of digital defense. MFA enhances the traditional username-password authentication by introducing additional layers of verification, making unauthorized access significantly more challenging for cybercriminals. This section delves into the realm of Multi-Factor Authentication, exploring its significance, mechanisms, benefits, challenges, and the art of its effective implementation.

Traditional password-based authentication has demonstrated vulnerabilities, often stemming from password reuse, weak passwords, and phishing attacks. MFA addresses these vulnerabilities by requiring users to provide multiple verification forms before granting access. These factors can entail something that the user knows (password), something that the user has (a physical token or smartphone), and something the user is (biometric data such as facial recognition or fingerprints). By combining these factors, MFA creates a formidable barrier against unauthorized access.

MFA introduces a layered approach to authentication, requiring users to present at least two of the verification factors mentioned earlier. When users attempt to log in, they provide their username and password as the first factor. Subsequently, they are prompted to provide the second factor, which could be a one-time code generated by an app, a text message, a hardware token, or a biometric scan. This dynamic combination ensures that even if a cybercriminal gains access to a user's password, they are thwarted by the additional layer of verification.

The primary benefit of MFA is its ability to enhance security significantly. Even if an attacker achieves to steal or guess a user's password, they would still require access to the second factor of verification, which is often a physical device or piece of information in the user's possession. This two-layered approach makes it exponentially more difficult for attackers to compromise an account. MFA also provides early warning signs of unauthorized access attempts, as users are immediately alerted when someone tries to log in using their credentials.

MFA is particularly effective in preventing unauthorized access resulting from password-related attacks. Phishing attacks, where attackers deceive users into divulging their passwords, become less impactful when MFA is in place. Additionally, MFA protects against brute-force attacks, where attackers systematically try various combinations of passwords. Even if a weak password is used, the second layer of verification acts as a robust safeguard.

While MFA offers significant security benefits, its implementation is not without challenges. User convenience is a consideration; some users might find the additional verification step cumbersome. Balancing security and usability is essential, Organizations must also educate their users about the importance of MFA and provide clear instructions on how to set it up. Training users to recognize legitimate MFA prompts and avoid phishing attempts is crucial.

Effective MFA implementation hinges on selecting the right factors for verification. A combination of convenient factors for users and providing strong security is ideal. For example, a common approach is combining something the user knows (password) with something they have (smartphone app generating one-time codes). Organizations can also leverage biometric data as a factor, further enhancing security.

MFA should be integrated into a broader cybersecurity strategy. It should not be the sole security measure but part of a layered defense. Coupled with strong password policies, regular security training, and other security mechanisms, MFA forms a formidable defense against a wide range of threats.

In a world where digital threats continue to evolve and data breaches make headlines, Multi-Factor Authentication stands as a robust shield, protecting individuals and organizations from unauthorized access. Its ability to thwart password-related attacks and enhance security without being overly intrusive makes it an essential component of modern cybersecurity. By embracing MFA and implementing it effectively, organizations elevate their digital defenses, empower their users with enhanced protection, and contribute to the broader effort of securing the digital landscape. As technology advances and cyber threats evolve, MFA remains a steadfast guardian, safeguarding access to the digital realm with a multifaceted approach that reflects the complexity of the modern threat landscape.

CHAPTER X

Incident Response and Recovery

Developing an Incident Response Plan

In the ever-evolving landscape of cybersecurity, the inevitability of facing cyber incidents has become a stark reality. From breaches on data to ransomware attacks, organizations of all sizes and industries are susceptible to the disruptive forces of cyber threats. Developing an Incident Response Plan (IRP) has emerged as a strategic imperative, offering a structured and proactive approach to effectively manage, contain, and mitigate the impact of cybersecurity incidents. An IRP outlines the processes, roles, and responsibilities guiding an organization's response to a security breach. This section delves into the realm of developing an Incident Response Plan, exploring its significance, key components, implementation strategies, challenges, and the critical role it plays in safeguarding digital assets and organizational reputation.

The digital age has brought unprecedented opportunities but has also ushered in a new era of cyber threats. From targeted attacks on sensitive data to sophisticated malware that can damage entire networks, the spectrum of potential incidents is vast and ever-expanding. An Incident Response Plan is designed to mitigate the consequences of these incidents by providing a structured approach to detect, respond to, and recover from security breaches. An effective IRP is not just about technical procedures; it encompasses communication strategies, coordination of stakeholders, and a clear roadmap for swift action in the face of adversity.

An effective IRP comprises several key components to ensure a comprehensive and well-coordinated incident response. The plan should define the roles and responsibilities of various stakeholders, from incident responders to communication personnel and legal advisors. It should outline the steps to identify and assess incidents, including categorization based on severity and impact. A well-structured IRP also includes predefined communication protocols, both internally and externally, to guarantee accurate and timely dissemination of information. Additionally, the plan should outline the steps to contain and mitigate the incident, recover affected systems and data, and conduct a post-incident analysis to identify lessons learned and areas for improvement.

Creating an IRP is not a solitary task; it requires collaboration across various organizational departments and stakeholders. The involvement of IT teams, legal experts, communication specialists, and senior management is essential to ensure that all facets of incident response are adequately addressed. This collaborative effort ensures the plan aligns with the organization's goals, policies, and risk tolerance. Developing an IRP is only the first step; its effectiveness lies in its execution. Regular testing and simulation exercises are crucial to ensure the plan is well-understood and can be executed efficiently during the chaos of an actual incident. Tabletop exercises, where stakeholders simulate incident scenarios and practice response strategies, offer valuable insights into the plan's effectiveness and identify areas that need refinement. Additionally, ongoing training for incident response team members is essential to update them on evolving threats, tools, and best practices.

Developing an effective IRP is not without challenges. One common obstacle is the dynamic nature of cyber threats; as threats evolve, the plan must adapt to address new attack vectors and tactics. The human factor also presents challenges; panic, miscommunication, or lack of coordination can hinder an effective response. Another challenge is balancing the need for speed and accuracy; responding swiftly is critical, but rushing without a well-defined plan can exacerbate the situation.

Incident response doesn't end when the incident is contained. Conducting a thorough post-incident analysis is crucial to identify what worked well and what requires improvement. This analysis informs updates to the IRP, helping the organization enhance its readiness for future incidents. It also provides valuable insights for stakeholders, allowing them to understand the incident's impact and the steps to address it.

In the dynamic realm of cybersecurity, where threats are constant and the consequences of incidents can be severe, an Incident Response Plan emerges as a guiding light in the face of adversity. It empowers organizations to navigate the unpredictable waters of cyber challenges with a well-coordinated, structured approach that minimizes damage, reduces downtime, and safeguards critical assets. By developing an effective IRP, organizations demonstrate their commitment to preparedness, resilience, and reputation protection. As technology advances and threats evolve, the IRP remains an essential tool, ensuring that the organization is equipped to respond with confidence, agility, and a strategic focus on minimizing the impact and restoring normalcy when cyber incidents strike.

Steps to Take During and After a Cyber Attack

The specter of cyber attacks looms large in the modern landscape of interconnected systems and digital transactions. From sophisticated ransomware assaults to data breaches that compromise sensitive information, organizations face an ever-evolving array of cyber threats. Responding effectively during and after a cyber attack is paramount to minimizing damage, restoring operations, and safeguarding sensitive data. This section delves into the critical steps that organizations should take during and after a cyber attack, providing a roadmap to navigate the tumultuous waters of digital threats and emerge stronger on the other side.

Chaos often reigns when a cyber attack unfolds, but a measured and strategic response is essential. First and foremost, isolate the affected systems from the network to hinder further spread of the attack. This may involve disconnecting affected devices or segments of the network. Simultaneously, engage the incident response team, comprising IT experts, legal advisors, communication specialists, and senior management. Clear communication is paramount; establish a central communication hub where all incident-related information is shared, documented, and analyzed.

Identify the nature and scope of the attack. Understanding the attack vector, the compromised systems, and the potential impact helps devise an appropriate response strategy. If the attack involves ransomware, assess the feasibility of decryption or data recovery options. Do not engage with attackers; seek guidance from law enforcement and cybersecurity experts.

Coordinate with external partners, like the law enforcement agencies and cybersecurity firms. Reporting the incident to the relevant authorities is crucial for legal and investigative purposes. Cybersecurity experts can assist in identifying the attack's origin, methods, and potential vulnerabilities exploited.

The journey to recovery and resilience begins as the dust settles after a cyber attack. Communicate transparently and promptly with stakeholders, including customers, employees, partners, and regulatory bodies. Public disclosure is often necessary, particularly if personal or sensitive data has been compromised. Provide accurate and transparent information about the incident, the steps taken to mitigate it, and the measures being implemented to prevent future occurrences.

Engage in a thorough post-incident analysis. Evaluate the incident response process to identify strengths and areas for improvement. This analysis informs the incident response plan updates, ensuring the organization is better prepared for future attacks.

Initiate a comprehensive assessment of the damage caused by the attack. Determine the extent of data loss, system compromise, and operational disruption. This assessment helps prioritize recovery efforts and informs decisions regarding data restoration or system rebuilds.

Restore affected systems and data. Depending on the severity of the attack, this process may involve wiping and rebuilding compromised systems, restoring data from backups, or decrypting data encrypted by ransomware. It's crucial to ensure that systems are clean and free from any lingering malicious code before bringing them back online.

After experiencing a cyber attack, organizations must prioritize enhancing their security posture and preparedness for the future. Implement lessons learned from the incident analysis into the incident response plan. Regularly test and update the plan to guarantee its effectiveness in the face of evolving threats.

Conduct a thorough review of the organization's cybersecurity measures. Identify vulnerabilities that were exploited during the attack and implement measures to address them. This may involve applying software patches, enhancing network segmentation, or bolstering access controls.
Invest in employee training and awareness programs. Often, cyber attacks exploit human vulnerabilities through tactics like phishing. Educating employees about cybersecurity best practices, recognizing suspicious activities, and adhering to security protocols is paramount.
Collaborate with cybersecurity experts to conduct a forensic analysis of the attack. Understanding how the attack occurred, the tools used, and the attacker's motivations provides insights that can guide future defenses.

In the ever-changing landscape of cyber threats, the ability to respond effectively during and after an attack is a litmus test of an organization's resilience. Navigating the storm of a cyber attack requires clear communication, strategic decision-making, and a coordinated response. Post-attack recovery involves restoring systems, mitigating damage, and bolstering defenses to prevent future breaches. By taking measured steps during and after an attack, organizations demonstrate their commitment to safeguarding their digital assets, protecting sensitive data, and emerging from the aftermath stronger, wiser, and better prepared to face the dynamic challenges of the digital age.

Learning from Incidents to Improve Security

In the intricate realm of cybersecurity, where threats are relentless and breaches are stark, organizations must adapt a proactive stance toward safeguarding their digital assets. Learning from incidents that have occurred, whether they are successful cyber attacks, near-misses, or vulnerabilities, has emerged as a cornerstone of building robust security strategies. These incidents serve as invaluable sources of information, offering insights into weaknesses, vulnerabilities, and areas that require improvement. This section delves into the practice of learning from incidents to improve security, exploring its significance, key benefits, challenges, and the transformative role it plays in enhancing an organization's overall cybersecurity posture.

Incidents, whether they result in successful breaches or near-misses, provide a wealth of information that can be harnessed to bolster an organization's security defenses. Every incident, be it a malware infection, a data breach, or a phishing attack, offers a unique opportunity for organizations to dissect and understand cybercriminals' tactics, techniques, and procedures. By analyzing incidents comprehensively, organizations can identify vulnerabilities, weaknesses in their defenses, and gaps in their incident response plans.

Learning from incidents provides many benefits that extend far beyond immediate breach mitigation. Incident analysis allows organizations to adapt and enhance their security measures based on real-world experiences. This proactive approach assists organizations to stay ahead of emerging threats and refine their strategies to counteract evolving attack vectors. The insights gained from incident analysis can be used to shape training programs, refine security policies, and guide technology investments to better align with actual risks.

Incident analysis provides organizations with an in-depth understanding of the various attack vectors employed by cybercriminals. Whether an attack involves exploiting software vulnerabilities, manipulating human psychology through social engineering, or leveraging insider threats, the incident sheds light on the methodologies used. This understanding enables organizations to focus on the most relevant security measures and countermeasures.
By learning from incidents, organizations can fine-tune their incident response strategies. Post-incident reviews offer insights into how well the response plan worked, areas that required improvement, and potential bottlenecks that hindered efficient mitigation. This iterative approach to incident response helps organizations build a resilient and efficient response framework, minimizing the impact of future incidents.
While learning from incidents offers significant advantages, there are challenges that organizations must navigate. One challenge lies in accurately capturing and documenting incident details. As incidents unfold, gathering relevant information and insights in real time is crucial, as post-incident assessments can be skewed if critical details are not documented promptly. Balancing the need for a thorough analysis with the urgency of responding to an incident can also pose a challenge.

Another challenge lies in handling sensitive information. Incidents often involve compromised data, and sharing or analyzing this data must be done with careful consideration of privacy regulations and data protection laws. Organizations must balance using incident data for learning purposes and protecting individuals' privacy.

Learning from incidents is most valuable when the insights gained are implemented effectively. Organizations should use incident analysis to improve their security policies, procedures, and technologies. Regularly updating security measures based on lessons learned ensures that the organization's defenses remain aligned with the evolving threat landscape.

Organizations must promote a culture of continuous improvement to truly leverage the power of learning from incidents. This involves encouraging open communication about incidents, emphasizing the importance of sharing lessons learned, and recognizing that every incident is an opportunity to enhance security practices. Organizations should create channels for incident reporting and analysis, ensuring that all relevant stakeholders are involved in the process.

In the digital age, where cyber threats are a constant and data breaches can have far-reaching consequences, learning from incidents becomes a catalyst for growth and resilience. Each incident, regardless of its severity, holds the potential to unveil vulnerabilities, refine response strategies, and guide future security investments. By embracing incidents as opportunities for learning, organizations transform adversity into strength, honing their security posture and equipping themselves to navigate the dynamic challenges of the digital landscape. In an environment where threats continue to evolve, learning from incidents is not just a reactive measure; it's a strategic approach that empowers organizations to proactively adapt, innovate, and emerge more robust in the face of adversity.

CHAPTER XI

Future Trends in Cybersecurity

Machine Learning and also Artificial Intelligence for Threat Detection

In the ever-evolving landscape of cybersecurity, where threats are dynamic and attacks are becoming increasingly sophisticated, the power of technology to combat these challenges has never been more apparent. Artificial Intelligence (also known as AI) as well as Machine Learning (also known as ML) have emerged as transformative forces in threat detection, revolutionizing how organizations identify and respond to cyber threats. By harnessing the capabilities of AI and ML, cybersecurity professionals can navigate the complexity of modern attacks, detect anomalies, and predict potential breaches with unprecedented accuracy. This section delves into AI and ML for threat detection, exploring their significance, mechanisms, benefits, challenges, and pivotal role in fortifying an organization's digital defenses.

A relentless barrage of attacks, from phishing and malware to ransomware and insider threats marks the modern threat landscape. Traditional security mechanisms, while valuable, struggle to keep up with the speed and complexity of these attacks. AI and ML provide a dynamic and adaptive approach to threat detection. Unlike rule-based systems that rely on predefined patterns, AI and ML systems learn from data and adapt their detection methods based on evolving attack techniques.

AI and ML systems analyze vast amounts of data to identify patterns and anomalies. This analysis enables them to detect subtle deviations from normal behavior, which could indicate the presence of a cyber threat. ML algorithms, such as supervised, unsupervised, and deep learning, process data to learn the characteristics of benign and malicious activities. Over time, these systems refine their models, improving their accuracy and reducing false positives.

The benefits of AI and ML in threat detection are manifold. These technologies significantly enhance threat detection accuracy, as they can identify patterns that might elude human analysts or rule-based systems. They also expedite detection, allowing organizations to respond swiftly to emerging threats. Furthermore, AI and ML systems adapt in real-time to changing attack vectors, providing a proactive defense against the dynamic nature of cyber threats.

One of the most potent aspects of AI and ML is their ability to detect unknown threats and zero-day vulnerabilities. These are threats that exploit vulnerabilities that are not yet known to the vendor or security community. AI and ML can identify anomalies in network traffic, user behavior, or system activity that could indicate a new and previously unseen threat.

While AI and ML offer remarkable benefits, they are not without challenges. One challenge lies in the potential for false positives or false negatives. Overly aggressive AI algorithms may flag legitimate activities as threats, while sophisticated attacks might evade detection. Striking the right balance between accuracy and precision requires careful tuning and training of the AI and ML models.

Another challenge is the data quality used to train AI and ML models. Biased or incomplete data can lead to skewed results and inaccurate predictions. Additionally, adversaries can employ adversarial techniques to manipulate AI models' behavior and evade detection.

AI and ML models may inadvertently infringe upon privacy rights, especially when analyzing personal or sensitive data. Striking a balance between effective threat detection and protecting privacy is a challenge that organizations must address.

The future of AI and ML in threat detection lies in integration and collaboration. These technologies should not replace human expertise but complement it. Human analysts are crucial in interpreting AI findings, refining models, and making critical decisions. Organizations should foster collaboration between cybersecurity professionals, data scientists, and AI experts to harness the full potential of these technologies.

In a digital landscape with relentless and ever-evolving threats, AI and ML are a force multiplier in cybersecurity defense. These technologies enable organizations to proactively identify and respond to threats with unprecedented accuracy and speed. By learning from data and adapting to emerging attack techniques, AI and ML provide a dynamic defense that can keep pace with the complexity of modern cyber threats. As technology develops and attacks become more sophisticated, the role of AI and ML in threat detection will continue to evolve, providing a robust and adaptable shield against the relentless tide of cyber adversaries. In embracing AI and ML, organizations equip themselves with the tools to navigate the intricate labyrinth of cybersecurity challenges and emerge more robust, more resilient, and better prepared to protect their digital assets.

Internet of Things (IoT) Security Challenges

The Internet of Things (IoT) has paved the way for a new era of interconnected devices, promising increased convenience, efficiency, and innovation. From smart homes as well as wearable devices to industrial automation and healthcare applications, IoT has the potential to revolutionize different aspects of our lives. However, this surge in connectivity also brings forth a complex web of security challenges that must be addressed to guarantee the safety and integrity of IoT ecosystems. This section delves into the multifaceted realm of IoT security challenges, exploring their significance, key dimensions, potential threats, and the imperative role of robust security measures in shaping the future of IoT.

The proliferation of IoT devices has transformed how we interact with technology and the world around us. These devices collect, exchange, and analyze data to deliver valuable insights and enhance our experiences. However, this data-driven connectivity also exposes critical vulnerabilities that cybercriminals can exploit. The significance of IoT security challenges lies in the potential for devastating consequences. Compromised IoT devices can lead to breaches of data, privacy infringements, and even physical harm. Securing IoT's vast and diverse landscape is paramount to realizing the full potential of this technology.
IoT security challenges are multidimensional, encompassing various layers of the technology stack.

Device security is a primary concern, as many IoT devices lack robust security measures due to resource constraints or rushed development. Communication security, including data transmission between devices and servers, is another critical dimension. Additionally, the management of device identities, secure software updates, and protecting user data all contribute to the intricate fabric of IoT security.

The IoT ecosystem presents many potential threats that can undermine its security and functionality. DDoS attacks can be magnified through the sheer number of interconnected devices, leading to massive disruptions. Unsecured communication channels can be intercepted, compromising the confidentiality of sensitive information. Unauthorized access to IoT devices can enable attackers to manipulate their behavior, resulting in physical damage or privacy breaches. Botnets, comprised of compromised IoT devices, can be used to launch large-scale cyber attacks.

One of the prominent IoT security challenges is the lack of robust authentication and authorization mechanisms. Many IoT devices rely on weak or default passwords, making them susceptible to brute-force attacks. Inadequate access control mechanisms can lead to unauthorized parties gaining control over devices or accessing sensitive data. The dynamic nature of IoT devices, often moving between different networks and environments, complicates the implementation of effective authentication and authorization protocols.

The vast amount of data generated and exchanged by IoT devices raises concerns about data security. Ensuring the confidentiality as well as integrity of data in transit is essential to prevent eavesdropping and tampering. Encrypting communication channels and employing secure protocols are critical measures. Additionally, securing data at rest within IoT devices and backend systems is crucial to prevent unauthorized access, especially given the potential sensitivity of the data collected.

IoT devices often gather vast amounts of personal data, raising concerns about user privacy. Users may not always be aware of the data collected, its use, and who has access to it. Establishing clear privacy policies, obtaining informed consent from users, and providing mechanisms for users to control their data are fundamental steps in addressing these challenges.

The complexity and scale of IoT environments pose significant security challenges. IoT ecosystems comprise a wide range of devices, each with varying capabilities and security requirements. Managing security across diverse devices, networks, and protocols is daunting. Furthermore, the lifecycle of IoT devices can span years, making it challenging to ensure ongoing security updates and patches.

Addressing the myriad IoT security challenges requires a collaborative effort from various stakeholders. Manufacturers must prioritize security in device design and development, embedding strong security measures from the outset. Standardization bodies can play a role in defining security guidelines and protocols for IoT devices. Government regulations and industry standards can establish minimum security requirements, fostering a culture of security-first IoT deployment.

The potential of IoT to reshape industries and enhance everyday life is undeniable, but this potential hinges on robust security measures that safeguard users, data, and critical infrastructure. Addressing IoT security challenges demands a multidimensional approach that spans device security, communication protocols, data protection, user privacy, and regulatory frameworks. As technology advances, the dynamic landscape of IoT security will evolve, requiring continuous adaptation and innovation to counter emerging threats. By recognizing the significance of IoT security challenges and proactively implementing comprehensive security measures, organizations and society at large can forge a future where the benefits of IoT are fully realized without compromising safety and privacy.

Ethical Considerations in Cybersecurity

In the intricate realm of cybersecurity, where the battle between attackers and defenders rages on, a vital underpinning often takes a back seat: ethics. The digital landscape is fraught with challenges that extend beyond the technical domain, raising complex ethical dilemmas that must be navigated with care. As organizations deploy defensive measures and governments enact policies to safeguard digital assets, ethical considerations are crucial in ensuring that protection aligns with principles. This section delves into the multifaceted realm of ethical considerations in cybersecurity, exploring their significance, key dimensions, potential conflicts, and their imperative role in shaping a secure and responsible digital future.

Cybersecurity is not solely about implementing firewalls and encryption; it encompasses the broader responsibility of safeguarding privacy, upholding human rights, and fostering trust. Ethical considerations in cybersecurity are essential because the actions taken to protect digital assets can have far-reaching consequences for individuals, organizations, and society at large. Balancing security imperatives with ethical principles ensures that cybersecurity measures do not infringe upon rights or violate norms.

Ethical considerations in cybersecurity encompass various dimensions that require careful assessment. Privacy is paramount, as cybersecurity measures often involve data collection and monitoring. Striking a balance between surveillance for protection and the right to privacy is a delicate endeavor. Transparency and accountability are also crucial; organizations must be transparent about their cybersecurity practices and accountable for their actions' impact on individuals and society.

Equity and inclusion in cybersecurity underscore the importance of ensuring that protective measures do not disproportionately affect certain groups or individuals. Cybersecurity policies that inadvertently discriminate or exclude specific populations raise ethical concerns and can perpetuate social inequalities. Ensuring that security measures are accessible, unbiased, and do not perpetuate systemic biases is vital.

Ethical considerations in cybersecurity can often collide with security imperatives. For instance, vulnerability disclosure is a complex ethical dilemma. Security researchers must decide whether to disclose a vulnerability, which could benefit attackers publicly. Striking a balance between responsible disclosure to help organizations patch vulnerabilities and preventing malicious exploitation is challenging.

Another ethical difficulty lies in the responsible use of offensive cybersecurity measures, often called "hack back" tactics. Retaliatory actions against attackers can lead to a cycle of escalation and may not align with principles of proportionality and legality. Determining when and how to respond to attacks without perpetuating harm requires careful ethical consideration.

Ethical or white-hat hacking involves testing systems for vulnerabilities to help organizations secure their assets. However, even ethical hacking raises questions about permission, boundaries, and the potential for unintended damage. Ethical hackers must navigate these considerations to ensure their actions are aligned with ethical principles.

Governments and industry bodies play a role in shaping ethical considerations in cybersecurity. Regulations and standards provide a framework for organizations to adhere to ethical principles. However, these regulations must balance security imperatives and privacy rights. Overly restrictive regulations can stifle innovation, while lax regulations can lead to security gaps.

New ethical considerations arise as emerging technologies like AI and IoT gain prominence. The potential for biased algorithms, invasive data collection, and unintended consequences amplifies the need for ethical guidelines. Ensuring that the deployment of these technologies aligns with ethical principles is paramount. The intricate tapestry of ethical considerations in cybersecurity underscores the need for a holistic approach that transcends technical prowess. As organizations and governments fortify digital defenses, it is imperative to remember that cybersecurity is not an end in itself but a means to uphold fundamental values and protect human rights. Ethical considerations guide developing and implementing cybersecurity measures, ensuring that the path to security is also a path of responsibility, transparency, and inclusivity. By prioritizing ethical principles in cybersecurity, organizations contribute to a digital landscape where protection and principles coexist, fostering trust, safeguarding rights, and paving the way for a secure and responsible digital future.

CHAPTER XII

Legal and Ethical Aspects of Cybersecurity

Data Privacy Regulations (e.g., GDPR, CCPA)

In an era characterized by the ubiquity of data and the rapid advancement of technology, the importance of data privacy has surged to the forefront of societal and regulatory agendas. As organizations gather, process, and share vast amounts of personal information, ensuring that individuals' privacy rights are respected has become paramount. The General Data Protection Regulation, better known as the GDPR, and the California Consumer Privacy Act (or CCPA), two data privacy laws, have become essential safeguards for individuals' personal information in the digital era. This section delves into the realm of data privacy regulations, exploring their significance, key provisions, global impact, challenges, and the evolving landscape of data protection.

Data privacy regulations are born from recognizing that personal information is a valuable asset that deserves protection. In an increasingly connected world, where data fuels innovations and drives decision-making, the potential for abuse and unauthorized use of personal data is substantial. Data privacy regulations aim to facilitate data-driven advancements and preserve individuals' privacy rights. These regulations codify principles that guide how organizations collect, store, process, and share personal information.

The GDPR, enacted by the European Union (EU) in 2018, and the CCPA, enacted in California, USA, in 2020, are prominent examples of data privacy regulations that have had a global impact. The GDPR emphasizes principles such as informed consent, the right to be forgotten, and data portability. It grants individuals greater control over their personal data, including accessing, rectifying, and deleting it. Similarly, the CCPA allows California residents to know what personal data or information is being collected about them, opt out of its sale, and sue for damages in case of data breaches.

Although the GDPR and CCPA are region-specific regulations, their impact extends beyond their geographic boundaries. The GDPR's extraterritorial reach affects any organization that processes the data of EU citizens, irrespective of its location. This has compelled numerous international organizations to reassess their data-handling practices to comply with GDPR provisions. The CCPA's influence is also felt globally as organizations that serve California residents must comply with its requirements, regardless of their headquarters location. The global nature of data flows and digital services has led to countries worldwide enacting similar regulations to protect their citizens' data.

While data privacy regulations are crucial for protecting personal information, but they also pose challenges for organizations and individuals. Organizations must navigate complex compliance requirements, which can be resource-intensive and necessitate changes in processes and technologies. The extraterritorial reach of regulations like the GDPR demands a global perspective on data privacy. Smaller businesses may struggle to implement the necessary measures to comply, potentially facing financial and reputational risks.

Another challenge lies in balancing data privacy and technological innovation. Regulations that impose stringent requirements can inadvertently stifle the development of data-driven technologies. Organizations must find ways to leverage data responsibly while respecting individuals' rights. Striking this balance requires collaboration between policymakers, technologists, and privacy advocates to ensure that innovation thrives without compromising privacy.

As technology evolves, so too must data privacy regulations. Emerging technologies which include artificial intelligence, the Internet of Things (IoT), and the processing of biometric data, provide new difficulties for the protection of individuals' privacy. Governments and regulatory bodies must continually update and adapt regulations to address these evolving threats. Furthermore, as data breaches and cyber attacks become more sophisticated, regulations must incorporate stringent data security measures to hinder unauthorized access to personal information.

In a digital landscape where personal information is both a commodity and a vulnerability, data privacy regulations are indispensable in safeguarding individuals' rights and fostering a climate of trust. Regulations like the GDPR and CCPA set a precedent for responsible data handling practices, giving individuals agency over their personal information and encouraging organizations to adopt transparent and accountable approaches. As data privacy considerations continue to gain prominence, stakeholders across sectors must recognize their role in navigating this complex landscape. By upholding the principles of data privacy and embracing the evolving standards set by regulations, organizations can contribute to a digital world where innovation coexists with responsible data practices, ensuring that the potential of technology is harnessed while preserving individuals' fundamental right to privacy.

Cybersecurity Ethics and Responsible Disclosure

In the digital age, where cyber threats are relentless and the stakes of security breaches are high, the importance of ethics in cybersecurity has become more evident than ever before. Cybersecurity professionals are tasked with protecting digital assets and upholding ethical principles that guide their actions. Among these principles, responsible disclosure is a cornerstone of ethical behavior, embodying the commitment to transparency, collaboration, and the greater good. This section explores the nexus of cybersecurity ethics and responsible disclosure, delving into their significance, key tenets, challenges, and the transformative role they play in shaping a secure and accountable digital landscape.

In the intricate realm of cybersecurity, where vulnerabilities are discovered, exploited, and patched, ethical considerations underpin the actions of professionals. Ethics in cybersecurity extend beyond mere technical competence; they encompass principles that govern the treatment of data, respect for privacy, and a commitment to the well-being of individuals and organizations. The significance of cybersecurity ethics lies in its ability to foster a culture of integrity, trust, and accountability. By adhering to ethical guidelines, cybersecurity professionals contribute to a digital ecosystem where protection and responsibility coexist. At the heart of cybersecurity ethics lies the principle of responsible disclosure, often called "ethical hacking." Responsible disclosure involves identifying security vulnerabilities in software, systems, or networks and then notifying the affected parties in a responsible and coordinated manner. The fundamental tenets of responsible disclosure include conducting thorough research, notifying the vendor or organization promptly, giving them adequate time to address the issue, and refraining from publicly disclosing the vulnerability until it is patched.

Responsible disclosure emphasizes collaboration over confrontation. Ethical hackers and security researchers collaborate with vendors to ensure that vulnerabilities are patched before they can be exploited maliciously. This collaborative approach enables organizations to address vulnerabilities without causing undue user harm or disruption.

Responsible disclosure requires striking a balance between disclosing vulnerabilities promptly and giving organizations sufficient time to develop and release patches. Rapid disclosure is essential to prevent potential exploitation, but it must be balanced against the need to provide organizations with adequate time to create effective solutions.

While responsible disclosure is a cornerstone of ethical behavior in cybersecurity, it is not without challenges. One challenge lies in the lack of clear guidelines and communication channels. Some organizations may lack a structured process for receiving and addressing vulnerability reports, leading to delays in patching. Another challenge arises from the potential conflict of interest between ethical hackers and organizations. While the intent is to enhance security, ethical hackers may have financial incentives tied to bug bounties or recognition for discovering vulnerabilities. This can sometimes lead to tensions over compensation and recognition.

Navigating the legal and ethical boundaries of responsible disclosure can also be challenging. Ethical hackers must ensure that their actions are within legal frameworks, especially if the act of probing for vulnerabilities could be interpreted as unauthorized access.

Responsible disclosure has a transformative power that extends beyond individual actions. It fosters a culture of transparency, accountability, and continuous improvement in the cybersecurity ecosystem. When vendors and organizations responsibly receive vulnerability reports, they are better positioned to address issues promptly, protect their users, and enhance their security posture.

Responsible disclosure also plays an educational role in cybersecurity. By sharing information about vulnerabilities and their remediation, ethical hackers contribute to the collective knowledge of the cybersecurity community. Information sharing helps others learn about new attack vectors, vulnerabilities, and best practices for mitigating risks.

In a digital landscape where the line between protection and exploitation is razor-thin, cybersecurity ethics and responsible disclosure principles shine as beacons of integrity. By adhering to ethical guidelines, cybersecurity professionals exemplify the values of transparency, collaboration, and responsible stewardship of technology. Responsible disclosure, in particular, demonstrates how the ethical use of skills and knowledge can elevate the security of digital ecosystems. As technology evolves, the role of ethical hackers and cybersecurity professionals in responsible disclosure becomes even more vital. By embodying these principles, they contribute to a secure, resilient, and ethical digital landscape that safeguards individuals, organizations, and society at large.

International Cooperation in Fighting Cybercrime

In an interconnected world driven by technology, the rise of cybercrime has transcended geographical boundaries, posing significant challenges to law enforcement and security agencies. The complexities of cyber threats, from ransomware attacks to data breaches, necessitate a collaborative global response leveraging international cooperation's power. The fight against cybercrime demands breaking down traditional borders and forging alliances that transcend national jurisdictions. This section explores the critical role of international cooperation in tackling cybercrime, its significance, key mechanisms, challenges, and the evolving landscape of collaborative efforts.

The interconnected nature of cyberspace has blurred the lines between domestic and international challenges. Cybercriminals operate in a borderless environment, exploiting vulnerabilities in one country to launch attacks on another. As a result, the significance of international cooperation in fighting cybercrime cannot be overstated. Collaborative efforts are essential to sharing intelligence, coordinating responses, and harmonizing legal frameworks across jurisdictions. By pooling resources, expertise, and knowledge, countries can develop a unified front against the global scourge of cybercrime.

International cooperation in fighting cybercrime is facilitated through various mechanisms, each tailored to address different dimensions of the challenge. Mutual Legal Assistance Treaties (MLATs) provide a framework for countries to request and provide assistance in criminal investigations and prosecutions. Cybersecurity information-sharing initiatives enable countries to exchange threat intelligence and best practices, enhancing collective situational awareness. International organizations like Interpol and Europol play a pivotal role in facilitating cross-border cooperation, and fostering collaboration among law enforcement agencies.

While international cooperation is essential, it has challenges. Cybercrime investigations' legal and jurisdictional complexities can hinder swift and effective cooperation. Differences in legal systems, data protection regulations, and interpretations of cybercrime can create obstacles to information sharing and evidence collection. Moreover, the rapid evolution of cyber threats demands agility in responses, which can be challenging when navigating bureaucratic processes.

Cultural and language barriers can also impede effective collaboration. Interpreting and translating technical information accurately can be challenging, leading to miscommunications and delays. Bridging these gaps requires building relationships and cultural awareness among international partners.
Geopolitical considerations can influence the willingness of countries to cooperate in cybercrime investigations. Issues of sovereignty, national security, and political tensions can impact the sharing of sensitive information. Striking a balance between national interests and the collective fight against cybercrime is a delicate endeavor. The landscape of international cooperation in fighting cybercrime continuously evolves to keep pace with emerging threats and technological advancements. Regional and bilateral agreements are expanding,

enabling countries to work together more effectively. Efforts to harmonize legal frameworks and standards are gaining traction, simplifying the process of sharing evidence and conducting joint investigations.

Public-private partnerships are emerging as a critical aspect of international cooperation. Collaborations between governments, law enforcement agencies, and private sector organizations can lead to more holistic and impactful responses to cyber threats. Private sector entities often possess unique insights and capabilities that can complement governmental efforts.

International cooperation also involves capacity building and technical assistance for developing nations. By sharing knowledge, providing training, and supporting the establishment of cybersecurity capabilities, developed countries can empower their counterparts to combat cybercrime effectively.

In an era where the digital realm knows no borders, the fight against cybercrime necessitates a united front that transcends national boundaries. International cooperation is a beacon of hope in the face of an evolving and dynamic threat landscape. Countries can pool their resources, leverage their expertise, and harmonize their legal frameworks to create a more secure and resilient digital environment by working together. While challenges persist, the collective resolve to combat cybercrime demonstrates the power of human collaboration to overcome adversity. As technology advances, the imperative of international cooperation in fighting cybercrime remains steadfast, reminding us that together, we can forge a safer, more secure digital future.

CONCLUSION

Recap of Key Strategies for a Secure Online Environment

As the digital landscape evolves, the imperative of a secure online environment becomes increasingly paramount. In a world where connectivity is ubiquitous and data is the currency of the digital realm, individuals, organizations, and governments alike must embrace a proactive and multi-faceted approach to safeguarding their online activities. This section summarizes the key strategies explored throughout this journey, outlining the fundamental principles, technologies, and practices that collectively contribute to fortifying the digital frontier.

At the core of any robust cybersecurity strategy lies the CIA Triad: Confidentiality, Integrity, and Availability. Confidentiality ensures that sensitive information is accessible only to authorized individuals, preventing unauthorized access. Integrity guarantees that data remains unaltered and accurate throughout its lifecycle. Availability ensures that systems and data are accessible and functional when needed, thwarting disruptions and downtime. Balancing these three pillars is essential for a comprehensive approach to cybersecurity.

The Principle of Least Privilege dictates that individuals and entities should only have access to the resources necessary to perform their tasks, minimizing potential damage from breaches. This principle dovetails with the Defense-in-Depth strategy, which involves layering multiple security measures to create a robust defense. By adopting a layered approach, organizations can thwart a wider array of attacks and ensure that if one layer is compromised, others stay intact.

Regularly updating software and promptly applying security patches is a critical practice to prevent exploits that take advantage of known vulnerabilities. By staying current with updates, organizations can proactively address security gaps that cybercriminals might attempt to exploit.

Secure password practices, including using strong, unique passwords and avoiding password reuse, are essential to preventing unauthorized access. Multi-factor authentication (MFA) further enhances security by requiring users to provide multiple verification forms. This ensures that even if a password is compromised, an additional layer of protection remains.

Employees play a pivotal role in cybersecurity; their awareness and education are paramount. Regular training programs that educate employees about phishing, social engineering, and best security practices empower them to effectively identify and respond to threats.

Firewalls are a barrier between internal networks and external threats, while Intrusion Detection Systems (IDS) monitor network traffic for suspicious activities. Virtual Private Networks (VPNs) provide encrypted tunnels for secure communication. Implementing these technologies adds an extra layer of security to online interactions.

Data encryption methods protect sensitive information from unauthorized access by converting it into unreadable code. Encrypting data at rest (when stored) and in transit (when transmitted) ensures that the data remains secure and unintelligible to attackers even if intercepted.

Ethical considerations in cybersecurity guide responsible behavior and respect for privacy. Responsible disclosure, or ethical hacking, involves reporting vulnerabilities to organizations in a coordinated and transparent manner. International cooperation is essential to combating cybercrime globally, transcending borders to share intelligence and resources.

The digital landscape is dynamic and ever-evolving, presenting both opportunities and challenges. The strategies outlined in this essay underscore the importance of proactive and multifaceted approaches to cybersecurity. Individuals and organizations can create resilient defense mechanisms by embracing principles like the CIA Triad, the Principle of Least Privilege, and Defense-in-Depth. Technologies such as firewalls, encryption, and VPNs bolster security measures, while training programs enhance human awareness and readiness. Ethical considerations, responsible disclosure, and international cooperation highlight the collaborative nature of cybersecurity. Collectively, these strategies form a comprehensive roadmap to fortify the digital frontier, ensuring that the benefits of the digital age are harnessed responsibly and securely. As technology evolves, the steadfast commitment to cybersecurity principles will pave the way for a secure and prosperous digital future.

Encouragement for Continuous Learning and Adaptation

In a world driven by technological advancements and digital transformation, the only constant is change. The rapid evolution of technology brings with it new opportunities, challenges, and risks that demand continuous learning and adaptation. Embracing a mindset of lifelong learning and also adaptability has become essential for personal and professional growth and navigating the ever-changing landscape of the digital age. This section delves into the importance of continuous learning and adaptation, its benefits, strategies for cultivating a learning mindset, and its role in shaping a successful and resilient future.

In an era characterized by the Fourth Industrial Revolution, where automation, artificial intelligence, and data-driven insights reshape industries, individuals must recognize that learning is not confined to formal education. Continuous learning is acquiring new knowledge, skills, and insights throughout one's life, driven by the recognition that staying relevant and effective requires ongoing adaptation to emerging trends and technologies.

Continuous learning offers many benefits, both on a personal and professional level. On a personal level, it enriches intellectual curiosity, enhances critical thinking, and promotes cognitive flexibility. Lifelong learners are better equipped to adapt to change, solve complex problems, and make informed decisions. Professionally, continuous learning fosters skill development, making individuals more versatile and resilient in a quickly evolving job market. It enhances career prospects, promotes innovation, and allows individuals to seize new opportunities as they arise.

Cultivating a learning mindset involves adopting strategies that embrace the philosophy of lifelong learning and adaptation. First and foremost, individuals must embrace curiosity and remain open to exploring new subjects, technologies, and ideas. Reading widely, attending workshops, and engaging in online courses are excellent ways to broaden one's horizons. Setting aside time for deliberate learning and creating a supportive environment that encourages exploration also play a crucial role in nurturing a learning mindset.

Adaptability complements continuous learning by enabling individuals to effectively apply their newfound knowledge and skills. In a rapidly changing environment, adaptability allows individuals to pivot when faced with challenges and seize opportunities that may not have been part of their initial plan. An adaptable mindset acknowledges that setbacks are opportunities for growth and innovation, motivating individuals to embrace change rather than resist it.

The digital age presents unique opportunities and challenges that underscore the importance of continuous learning and adaptability. Technological advancements like AI and automation are reshaping industries and redefining job roles. Those who adapt to these changes by acquiring relevant skills are more likely to thrive. Moreover, the digital age facilitates learning through online platforms, enabling individuals to access a wealth of resources and expertise from the comfort of their homes.
While the benefits of continuous learning are evident, barriers such as time constraints, financial limitations, and a fear of failure can hinder progress. Overcoming these barriers needs a shift in mindset and recognizing that investing in one's learning journey is an investment in personal and professional growth. Leveraging online resources, forming learning communities, and seeking out mentorship can help individuals overcome these challenges.

In a world characterized by quick technological advancements and constant change, the journey of continuous learning and adaptation is not a luxury but a necessity. Embracing this journey empowers individuals to remain relevant, agile, and prepared to thrive in a dynamic environment. Continuous learning sharpens cognitive abilities, enriches personal experiences, and broadens horizons. Adaptability ensures that the acquired knowledge and skills are applied effectively, allowing individuals to navigate challenges and seize opportunities. As the digital landscape evolves, those who embrace lifelong learning and adaptability are poised to create a successful and resilient future. The journey may be challenging, but the rewards of personal growth, professional success, and the fulfillment of realizing one's potential make it a path worth traversing.

Emphasizing Individual and Collective Responsibility

In a world that is increasingly interconnected and reliant on technology, the concept of responsibility has taken on new dimensions. The digital age has ushered in unparalleled opportunities and challenges, requiring individuals and societies to recognize the importance of individual and collective responsibility. As technology intertwines with every facet of our lives, our actions' ethical, social, and environmental consequences have become more profound. This section delves into the significance of emphasizing individual and collective responsibility in the digital age, exploring the implications, benefits, challenges, and strategies for fostering a culture of accountability.

Responsibility in the digital age extends beyond traditional notions of personal duty. The rapid pace of advancement in technology, coupled with the pervasive reach of the digital realm, has magnified the impact of individual actions on a global scale. From data privacy breaches to the ecological footprint of digital infrastructure, our choices in the digital sphere reverberate far beyond our immediate surroundings. Recognizing and embracing responsibility in this context is essential for addressing ethical dilemmas, promoting sustainable practices, and ensuring the well-being of individuals, societies, and the planet.

Individual responsibility in the digital age encompasses various dimensions. Data privacy, for instance, underscores the importance of users safeguarding their personal information and being vigilant about how their data is collected, used, and shared. Digital citizenship involves respecting others' online identities and engaging in respectful, ethical behavior in digital spaces. The ethical use of emerging technologies like AI and biometrics demands careful consideration of their societal impact. Embracing individual responsibility also involves reducing digital pollution, such as minimizing e-waste and energy consumption.

While individual responsibility is crucial, the complexity of the digital ecosystem necessitates a collective approach. The interdependence of technology and society calls for collaboration among individuals, organizations, governments, and international bodies to address pressing issues. Collective responsibility involves holding corporations accountable for ethical practices, advocating for policy changes, and working together to mitigate the negative implications of technological advancement.

Emphasizing individual and collective responsibility yields a host of benefits. On an individual level, it empowers people to be proactive agents of change, fostering a sense of agency and ownership over the digital landscape.

Collectively, a culture of responsibility creates a shared commitment to ethical conduct, driving positive societal change. Responsible use of technology also contributes to the sustainability of digital resources, reduces digital divides, and enhances the quality of online interactions.

Promoting responsibility in the digital age is challenging. The rapid pace of technological change can outpace societal norms and regulations, leading to gaps in accountability. Navigating complex ethical dilemmas, such as AI bias or deepfake manipulation, requires multifaceted solutions that engage stakeholders from various sectors. Additionally, the global nature of the digital ecosystem requires a coordinated effort among nations to develop common frameworks for responsible behavior.

Fostering responsibility involves a multi-pronged approach encompassing education, awareness, regulation, and collaboration. Educational initiatives can provide individuals with the knowledge and skills needed to make responsible decisions in the digital realm. Awareness campaigns highlight the consequences of irresponsible behavior, encouraging individuals to reflect on their choices. Regulation plays a crucial role in setting standards and expectations for ethical conduct, while collaboration among governments, industry leaders, and civil society fosters a shared commitment to responsible practices.

In an era where technology is integral to daily life, responsibility has acquired new dimensions and implications. The digital age calls for a paradigm shift, where individuals recognize the impact of their digital choices and take ownership of their roles as digital citizens. Emphasizing individual and collective responsibility is not just a moral imperative but a pathway to a sustainable, ethical, and prosperous digital future. By making conscious choices, promoting ethical conduct, and advocating for responsible practices, individuals and societies can navigate the intricacies of the digital age with integrity and accountability. The journey toward a responsible digital future is a collective endeavor that transcends borders, sectors, and generations, reflecting our shared commitment to shaping a world where technology serves as a force for good.